THE RIGHT CHURCH

THE RIGHT CHURCH

Live Like the First Christians

Charles E. Gutenson

Abingdon Press
Nashville

THE RIGHT CHURCH: LIVE LIKE THE FIRST CHRISTIANS

Cataloging-in-Publication Data has been requested with the Library of Congress

ISBN 978-1-4267-4911-7

12 13 14 15 16 17 18 19 20 21—10 9 8 7 6 5 4 3 2 1

MANUFACTURED IN THE UNITED STATES OF AMERICA

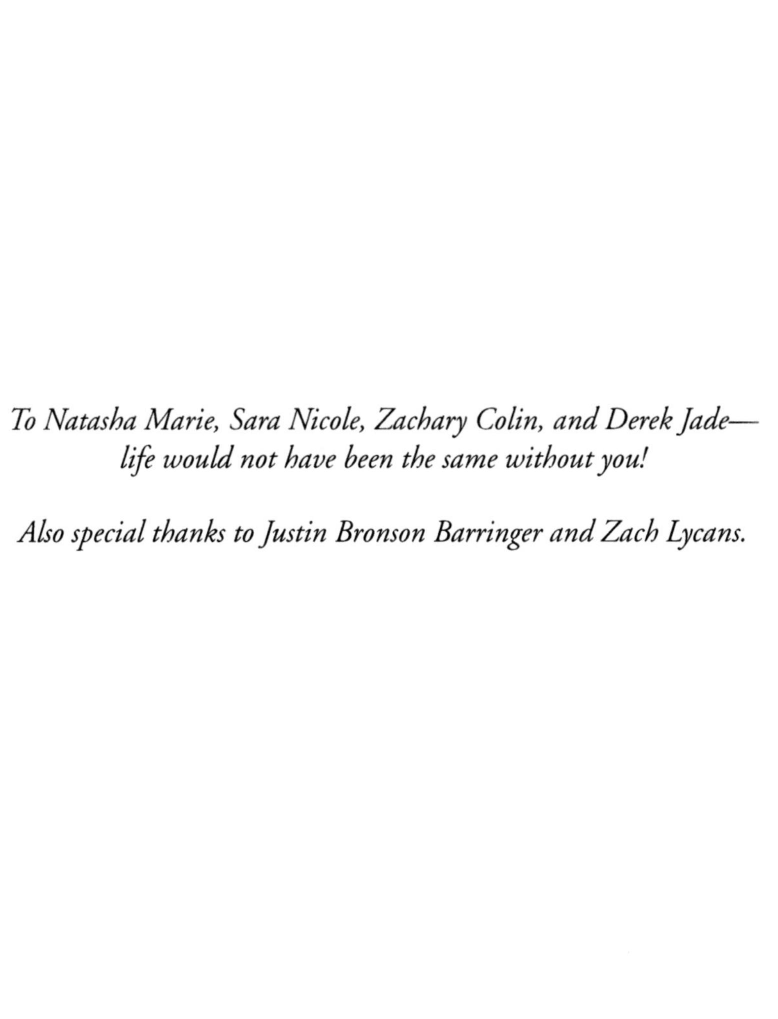

To Natasha Marie, Sara Nicole, Zachary Colin, and Derek Jade—
life would not have been the same without you!

Also special thanks to Justin Bronson Barringer and Zach Lycans.

CONTENTS

INTRODUCTION

If you were to ask my greatest passion, the answer would only require two words—church renewal. The state of the church in the contemporary United States has me deeply concerned. There are, of course, local congregations engaged in many wonderful ministries across the country. So all is not lost. Yet, study after study by noted pollster George Barna demonstrates the shockingly small difference the church makes in how we live. By now, he has assessed some seventy different behaviors, comparing non-Christians with those who self-profess as followers of Jesus. He has yet to find much significant difference between the two groups. Think about that for a moment: seventy different behavioral traits, and the differences exhibited by self-identified Christians and non-Christians is negligible. In fact, if you dig into the details,[1] there are some cases where non-Christians actually outperform Christians—charity and care for what the Christian Scriptures call "the least of these," for example. A Christian band named DC Talk once introduced a song with this quotation:

> The greatest single cause of atheism in the world today is Christians who acknowledge Jesus with their lips then

> walk out the door and deny him by their lifestyle. That is what an unbelieving world simply finds unbelievable.

So, yes, my greatest passion is church renewal, to see the church renewed so that it begins to make a difference in how followers of Jesus live—specifically, to see us live more like Jesus.

One might say that I should just give up on the church. God can impact the lives of followers of Jesus any way God chooses, right? So, why not look for other means to accomplish changed lives? The answer is simple and straightforward. Jesus is the hope of the world, and Jesus has chosen to use the church as the means by which that hope is modeled and proclaimed in the world. For me, there is no giving up on the church. There might be disappointment, criticism, and frustration at times, but these are all born out of love for the church. So there can be no giving up, at least not for me.

At one level, then, this book is about church renewal. In a sense, it is about going forward by looking back, a desire to awaken the church of today by appealing to the church of yesterday, and not just any yesterday, but all the way back to the earliest church period—the period closest to the life of Jesus. The question that lies behind this study is this: how did the early church understand the nature of faithful discipleship? And, then, how should that impact and influence how we live today?

There's a good deal of mythology and romanticism about the earliest period of the church. Some perhaps believe the prescription for the contemporary church's ailments is found in a recovery of the supposed purity of the "early church." This book is not a romantic inquiry into the "golden days" of the church, but rather an attempt to crack open a window into the early church. Our purpose is to examine how differently early Christians saw the world. My hope is not that the reader will walk away agreeing with everything one might find in that early period. I do hope, though, that it might inspire some lively debate and that the Spirit might use that debate to sow seeds of renewal in the church. A renewal that will change us so that when the world looks at the church, it sees a genuine and distinct alternative "way of being"—one more consistent with the life lived by our Lord.

We as Christians are heirs to a remarkably rich tradition dating back at least two thousand years, much longer when you include the prior Jewish tradition from which Christianity sprang. Within that history, we find different understandings of what it means to be faithful to God's call upon our lives, and more specifically, how following Jesus is supposed to be lived out. Perhaps some of those ways of following Jesus stand in a degree of tension with others. Yet part of the wisdom of the church has been its willingness to allow those tensions to stand side by side. In this way, the differences challenge us to think more carefully rather than giving the tensions an easy resolution. Origen once observed something similar about the Scriptures themselves. He was convinced that God allowed tensions to stand within the text because God knew that a key part of our formation was intimately connected with our sorting those tensions within communities of faith. It seems Origen believed that God was interested not so much in "blind obedience" as he was in folks who could "think theologically." Not every possible circumstance we might face in life is directly addressed in Scripture. So, if we will but let them, Scripture and tradition can stand as dual mentors in developing our ability to move beyond following the "letter of the law" to living in a way that makes us better followers of our Lord.

Unfortunately, for the vast majority of Christians, this deep and rich heritage, for all practical purposes, does not exist. Why? Well, the short answer is: ignorance or perhaps more simply, unawareness. If it is the case that we, as a group, are becoming increasingly ignorant of the biblical narratives themselves (and it almost certainly is the case), it is even more the case that we are ignorant of the rich heritage of the church. In that heritage, we find resources available for working out how best to be faithful followers of Jesus in our contemporary context. Most Christians today would consider themselves well read if they have managed to stay plugged in to the contemporary Christian scene—reading relatively contemporary books and listening to sermons and scriptural commentary from the last, oh, say, fifty years. I expect some in my own United Methodist tradition would consider themselves remarkably well read if they had actually worked their way through some of John Wesley's fifty-two standard sermons. Yet, as old and as rich as those sermons are, they reach back not even three hundred years—a very short time when compared to the multi-millennium history of the church.

A rallying cry during the Middle Ages was *ad fontes*, which means "back to the fountain" or "back to the origins." The idea was that Christians needed to get back to the early church period to recapture the vibrant faith exhibited during that period. It is time again to cry out "Ad fontes!" and to turn our attention more intentionally to the wisdom of the early church, to its preachers and its bishops. Not necessarily because we will always agree with them, not because we buy into that myth of a pure, early church, but because it is vitally important to us today to consider how Christians of different time periods have sought to be faithful. We need to look beyond the mythology of the early church and discover what the early church wrote and, more importantly, how the early church *lived.*

In response to my comments about the importance of reading the early church fathers and mothers, an acquaintance once said that he could not understand why he would take the time to read all that. Why spend so much time on an activity that would leave him with the same theology he already had? I was nonplussed. If a person takes the time to examine the early church writings and finds his or her theology and practice unchanged, I suspect it can only be because he or she was not paying attention. How many know what Irenaeus had in mind when he said, "This is my Gospel"? Did he mean one of the four Gospels was his favorite? (By the way, that's not what he meant.) How many of us can repeat the words of Gregory when he commented on the authority of Basil's commentary on Genesis? How many know what words of warning St. John Chrysostom had to issue to those who were well-to-do and how many can recite the obligations that he claimed attended wealth? Did you know that prior to the close alignment between Emperor Constantine and the church, the overwhelming position that the church held on issues of war and peace was pacifist? Augustine was a great defender of the faith, contributing mightily to the church's unfolding understanding of the Trinitarian nature of God. How many are aware of his contributions to how Christians see issues of wealth and poverty? In our contemporary world, there is much justified concern about how well we are relieving our obligations to steward the planet that God has entrusted to us. How many realize that even in the early church period bishops were preaching about our obligations to care for the world God has created? In the course of our study, we will examine these and many more of the claims made within the early church, claims that will sound strange to our twenty-first-century ears, but claims we ought, nevertheless, to hear.

Are we unaware of earlier parts of our heritage for reasons of chronological snobbery—that is, since we are the latest generation, we must be the best informed, thinking that the early church has little useful to say to us? Or, is it just because the quantity of materials is so vast that one hardly knows where to start? Or, perhaps it is simply that the pace of contemporary life is so frenzied that we seem rarely to have time available for such luxuries as examination of our rich Christian heritage. Whatever the reason, I dare say that few, if any, who have taken the time to explore those riches have come away disappointed.

Consider an example of the benefit of better understanding the different expressions of Christian faith. When I was a youngster, there was a particular point at which, even as a teen, I found myself coming to very different theological conclusions than those drawn by my denomination. Of course, I viewed our pastors and teachers as "the experts," and I was sure that I was misreading the Bible. And, while I could never quite understand the reading my denomination held, I tried my best to believe it was correct. Sadly, my inability to do so was quite often a source of doubt and concern for me, an indicator of my substandard faith. Well, you can imagine my surprise (and, to be honest, my relief!) when later exposure to other denominations made it clear that the position my denomination had held was a minority opinion and that the bulk of the tradition had read the passages as I had. None of this, of course, proved which reading was actually true; what it did was demonstrate to me that followers of Jesus have often come to different conclusions about biblical teaching on many points and that the tradition was broad enough to accommodate many of those differences.

In the course of teaching a number of classes over the years, I have found myself often offering students little tidbits from the early church that aimed to show them how different followers of Jesus have understood what it meant to be faithful. Foremost, my goal in this book is to illuminate these differences. I do not intend to treat the early church writings as if they are normative or proscriptive for how all Christians should live. For example, while I do not use this example in what follows, one could present some of Basil's denials of personal ownership of property and say, "See, since Basil thought property ownership was wrong, Christians should not own property." My goal is much more modest. In some cases and for some persons, perhaps God's Spirit will use these words to kindle a deeper passion for imitating Jesus and, in turn, create a pocket of renewal within the church. In other cases, perhaps that same Spirit will help us see that some positions we have rejected do, after all, fit under the umbrella of Christian faith. In all cases, it is my hope that our study together will intrigue you enough to devise a way to make study of the broader, richer Christian tradition a part of your own life of faith. In so doing, we risk nothing but the loss of our ignorance and the chance to gain a depth of faith that we would miss otherwise.

My approach is twofold. First, I can give you some pictures into the lives of discipleship of several from the early church period. I can describe the positions they held, and in many cases, help you see why they held them. In short, I can tell you how some of your Christian brothers and sisters have understood being faithful to the gospel and offer an opportunity to examine together some of the acts of discipleship they thought critical to being faithful. Second, I can encourage you to ask honestly how these teachings and actions impact your own understanding of what it means to be a faithful follower of Jesus. So, while I cannot say to you, "Ambrose did this, and you should, too," I can say, "Your brother Ambrose, who lived in a different time and place, felt that these particular acts were essential to faithful discipleship. What can we learn from Ambrose and what ought we to do about it?"

Structurally, each chapter will contain sayings from the early church. Having some context about the identities of our different conversation partners will be important. However, if I introduce them all in the first chapter, we will get bogged down in too much church history and too little examination of the words we have come to consider. So, I will offer some context for one of the persons from the early church in each chapter. By the end, you will have some context for many, while allowing each chapter the freedom to stay focused on its particular topic.

With that in mind, let us take a look at some of the early church's statements that challenge our normal, twenty-first-century way of seeing things. Let the fun begin!

Part One: Church Life

I.

Reading Scripture with the Early Church

In many Protestant traditions, after the Scriptures have been read for the worship service, it is not unusual to hear the words, "The Word of God for the people of God." Often one hears the response, "Thanks be to God!" In the Eastern Orthodox tradition, one can expect to hear words such as, "Wisdom, let us attend," prior to or following the reading of the Bible. In some churches, when the particular reading is from the Gospels, the congregation is asked to stand. In yet others, an open Bible is carried aloft as part of the procession that opens worship while the congregation stands. In still others, the reader, the congregation, or both give some physical sign of respect at the conclusion of the scriptural reading. All of these actions, whether words recited or physical enactment, are signs we use to demonstrate our respect for the most holy of Christian texts—the Bible. While the precise way in which we show our respect and the exact nature of the language we use to state our commitment varies, the Christian Scriptures universally occupy a unique and special place across the Christian faith.

Christians have tried in various ways to capture the uniqueness of the Scriptures in doctrinal statements. For example, terms such as *inerrant* or *infallible* have been used to emphasize the trustworthiness of the Scriptures. In some cases, these terms have been applied broadly to anything that might be addressed in the Bible, whether directly or tangentially related to the life of faith. Others have been more carefully nuanced, applying the terms only to matters specifically related to human salvation and restoration of right relationship to God. Still others within the broader Christian tradition have found that these particular terms have become too charged and have opted instead for terms like *authoritative.* Some have tried to focus on the role of the Scriptures in defining what constitutes the faithful life by saying things like, "The Scriptures are normative for all things related to Christian conversion and discipleship." While allowing different strands of the faith to express their allegiance to the Scriptures in the way they feel best, the common point is the same: the Christian Bible holds a unique place for us as followers of Jesus. Throughout the centuries, when it comes to discerning what God would have God's people do, there is nothing to which appeal has been more often made than to the collection of writings Christians call the Scriptures.

The Beginnings of Scripture

Unfortunately, most of us are only familiar with the ways in which the Scriptures have been understood over the last hundred or so years. Early church writings have much to enrich our grasp of them, or perhaps better, to enrich their grasp on us. For example, unless one has taken the time to study the first centuries of church history, one is unlikely to know how the collection of writings we call the Christian Bible even came into existence. Sometimes, we seem almost to operate on the idea that they dropped from heaven with God's name on a signature line. Of course, it was not so. Hans van Campenhausen, in what is still considered by many to be the most significant book on the subject, *The Formation of the Christian Bible,*[1] notes that it was A.D. 200 or later before the books of either the Old Testament or the New Testament were reasonably settled. The final determination came even later.

It is impossible to separate the Scriptures from the early church's work, under the guidance of the Holy Spirit, by which they were identified. I recall a student once asking me to work with him on an independent study. His stated goal was to "get behind the early church fathers, so one could hear the words of Scripture alone." My response was that I did not see how we could do that. How do you get behind the work of the early church when it was the early church that identified what constitutes the Christian Scriptures? Further, it would seem quite strange to affirm that God had guided the early church to correctly identify the books (which we affirm when we speak of the Bible as God's Word), but not to affirm that God equally guided their judgments about what the Bible meant. To recognize this should in no way undermine our confidence in the Scriptures. Rather, it should elevate our appreciation for the early church and God's work in guiding it. Were the Scriptures inspired by God? Absolutely, they were inspired to be authoritative regarding the life of faith. Perhaps, though, we would do well to imitate the early church, which affirmed the unique place of the Scriptures as God's inspired revelation without feeling it necessary to say definitively *how* they were inspired.

The first time that the twenty-seven books currently taken to constitute the New Testament show up, all together in an authoritative statement, is in the Festal Letter of Athanasius in the year A.D. 367. Many are surprised to hear that the Christian church had been functioning for nearly four centuries before the final form of the New Testament was settled. Here is how Athanasius put it (just before this quotation, he had listed the Old Testament books):

> Continuing, I must without hesitation mention the Scriptures of the New Testament; they are the following: the four Gospels according to Matthew, Mark, Luke, and John, after them the Acts of the Apostles and the seven so-called catholic epistles of the apostles—namely, one of James, two of Peter, then three of John and after these one of Jude. In addition there are fourteen epistles of the apostle Paul written in the following order: the first to the Romans, then two to the Corinthians and then after these the one to the Galatians, following it the one to the Ephesians, thereafter the one to the Philippians and the one to the Colossians and two to the Thessalonians and the epistle to the Hebrews and then immediately two to Timothy, one to Titus and lastly the one to Philemon. Yet further the Revelation of John.[2]

Regarding the role of these Scriptures, along with those of the Old Testament, Athanasius leaves no doubt:

> These are the springs of salvation, in order that he who is thirsty may fully refresh himself with the words contained in them. In them alone is the doctrine of piety proclaimed. Let no one add anything to them or take anything away from them.[3]

He does not stop with this list of texts, but goes on to recognize the importance of certain other writings to salvation and the life of faith:

> But for the sake of greater accuracy I add, being constrained to write, that there are also other books besides these, which have not indeed been put in the canon, but have been appointed by the Fathers as reading-matter for those who have just come forward and [wish] to be instructed in the doctrine of piety. . . .[4]

Already we see an important number of points. First, it is fascinating to reflect on how God, through the Holy Spirit, was guiding the growth of the church at the same time as God was directing the canonical process whereby the church's authoritative writings were identified. Second, we find in Athanasius in particular and the early church more generally a very winsome connection between the Scriptures and human salvation. Metaphors such as used here ("springs of salvation, in order that he who is thirsty may fully refresh himself") are frequent. People, to use Matthew's words, "are hungry and thirsty for righteousness," and it is in the Scriptures that they are fed and their thirst is sated. Third, while the canonical books are afforded a special place amongst Christian writings, Athanasius is but one of the early fathers who remind us of other books appointed by the church to serve in the deepening life of faith and discipleship. The strong distinction between the Scriptures and other holy writings would be the product of a much later age.

Ways of Reading Scripture

Perhaps one of the most prolific theologians and biblical scholars of the early church was Origen. His work *On First Principles* was one of the earliest to develop a more formal biblical hermeneutic. As John McGuckin notes, "Origen is not the originator of the idea of a biblical canon, but he certainly gives the philosophical and literary-interpretative underpinnings for the whole notion."[5] Origen was born around 184/5, probably in Alexandria to Christian parents. His father, Leonides, provided his education. He made sure Origen had access to the standard educational fare of the day, but in addition, saw to it that Origen was trained in the Scriptures. As with Basil the Great (whom we meet later), Origen's father was martyred for his faith during a period of Christian persecution under Septimius Severus in 202. Origen's passions were stirred at the death of his father so that he desired to join him in martyrdom. In an interesting twist, Origen's mother saved him for us by hiding his clothes so that he could not leave. While the family fell into poverty at the death of Leonides, Origen was able to survive by a life of extreme asceticism and, initially, the income generated by the sale of his library. He went on to become an exceptional scholar of the Christian faith. The bulk of his teaching career was spent in Alexandria.

As we move into Origen's writings on the Scriptures, let us begin with his idea that they must be read in a "threefold" way. Consider this quotation from Book IV of *First Principles:*

> The right way, therefore, as it appears to us, of approaching the scriptures and gathering their meaning, is the following, which is extracted from the writings themselves. We find some such rule as this laid down by Solomon in the Proverbs concerning the divine doctrines written therein: "do thou portray them threefold in counsel and knowledge, that thou mayest answer words of truth to those who question thee."

> One must therefore portray the meaning of the sacred writings in a threefold way upon one's own soul, so that the simple man may be edified by what we may call the flesh of scripture, this name being given to the obvious interpretation; while the man who has made some progress may be edified by its soul, as it were, and the man who is perfect and like those mentioned by the apostle: "we speak wisdom among the perfect; yet a wisdom not of this world, [nor] of the rulers of this world, which are coming to nought; but we speak God's wisdom in a mystery, even the wisdom that hath been hidden, which God foreordained before the worlds unto our glory"—this man may be edified by the spiritual law, which has "a shadow of the good things to come." For just as man consists of body, soul, and spirit, so in the same way does the scripture, which has been prepared by God to be given for man's salvation.[6]

In short, then, Origen's idea is that the Scriptures have a "bodily" meaning, a "soulish" meaning, and a "spiritual" meaning, each of which is intended to be understood by Christians as they grow deeper in their faith. But *how* do these three levels of meaning help us better understand the Scriptures and be formed by our interaction with them?

Interpreters of Origen have generally taken the three senses of the Scriptures as follows. First, the "bodily" meaning is just what the text appears to say—its "literal" meaning, if you will. When we are told that Jesus was born in Nazareth, the meaning of the text is clear. Or, when we are told that Jesus was tried before Pilate, the "bodily" or "literal" sense is immediately clear. Second, the "soulish" sense of the Scriptures relates to its moral truths or the application of their moral teachings. However, this second, or "soulish," meaning receives relatively little direct attention in Origen. More frequently, the second and third (or "spiritual") meanings get combined into a broader distinction in Origen, the distinction between the "letter" and the "spirit" of the biblical writings. The "spiritual" meaning relates to the deeper truths. Often, these point to Christ, as when he notes Paul's statement that the rock Moses struck to obtain water for the Israelites referred to Christ. Sometimes, the spiritual meaning, when properly grasped, reveals the truths of church doctrine—such as the trinitarian doctrine or the doctrines related to Jesus' nature. As we noted, though, the "soulish" and "spiritual" meanings are often joined together over against the "bodily" meaning. The resulting distinction is, then, between the literal/bodily meanings and those that are more hidden, nonliteral meanings.

Notably, Origen did not feel constrained to defend a literal interpretation of every biblical passage, a tendency that we more frequently find much later. Origen noted that some passages were not intended to be read literally at all:

> But since there are certain passages of scripture, as we shall show in what follows, [that] have no bodily sense at all, there are occasions when we must seek only for the soul and the spirit, as it were, of the passage.[7]

Starting in the next chapter of his work, Origen outlines several passages that he believes do not have a bodily sense.[8] How do we recognize these passages that are not to be taken literally? Origen says that they are the ones that are impossible or unreasonable or somehow convey something unworthy of God—something that would call the character of God into question:

> But someone may suppose that the former statement refers to all the Scriptures, and may suspect us of saying that because some of the history did not happen, [then] none of it happened; and because a certain law is irrational or impossible when taken literally, therefore no laws ought to be kept to the letter; or that the records of the Savior's life are not true in the physical sense; or that no law or commandment of his ought to be obeyed. We must assert, therefore, that in regard to some things we are clearly aware that the historical fact is true.[9]

In fact, he goes on to say:

> For the passages which are historically true are far more numerous than those which are composed with purely spiritual meanings.[10]

So, broadly speaking, though Origen affirmed that the Scriptures had a threefold meaning—the bodily, the soulish, and the spiritual—one can think of his work as identifying two overarching categories. The first of these is the literal sense of the Scriptures—the meaning that one gets from the meanings of the words themselves. Sometimes this is called the "letter" of the biblical writings. The second is the nonliteral meaning—the meaning that one gets when one looks past the surface, "literal" meaning and probes deeper. Not all of the Scriptures have a literal/bodily meaning, though all of the Scriptures have a spiritual meaning. When there is a literal meaning (and Origen affirms this is most frequently the case), that meaning is edifying and instructive for the person of faith. As we grow in faith, Origen believed, we become able to grasp the deeper meaning, which is appropriately edifying for those at that stage of Christian growth.

Wrestling with Scripture

It might be appropriate to ask the role of the Scriptures in the life of faith, at least as far as Origen saw it. It is fair to say that he did not combine "conversion of life" and "salvation" as if they were one and the same thing. In other words, Origen would have argued that the goal of the Scriptures is to form us into the people of God, into a people who live out with integrity the life of faith. To that end, he believed that the Scriptures say what God intended them to say. However, consistent with his understanding of their goal of the conversion of life, he recognized the importance of our "wrestling" with the Scriptures, having to dig deep to get all the meaning. It is precisely in that struggle that they do their formative work on us. They lead not just to our faith in the sense of rightly believing, but also to our faith in the sense of rightly living—that is, nothing short of the full conversion of life.

Origen recognized that sorting between those passages that had a literal meaning and those that did not would often be complicated. He knew that there might be cases where the student of the Scriptures may easily be able to tell that the passage at hand does not have what he called a bodily meaning. In fact, as noted above, he gave several examples. There may also be passages where it is equally easy to tell that a given passage has a bodily meaning, and we have already noted that he considered these to be the majority. At the same time, he recognized that there would be cases where we find ourselves "unable to decide, without considerable investigation whether a particular incident, believed to be history, actually happened or not, and whether the literal meaning of a particular law is to be observed or not."[11] Notice, however, what Origen does not do: (1) he does not caution us about a "slippery slope" that arises from questioning the historicity of any passage, (2) he does not resolve the tension easily in either direction (that is, he does not have a default position that assumes a passage to be historical or not), and (3) he does not lose his respect for the authority of the Scriptures over our lives.

So, what was the outcome? How did Origen think we are to proceed?

> . . . the [person] who reads the divine books reverently believing them to be divine writings, must exercise great care.[12]

We have probably all encountered those who believe that the only way to take the Scriptures seriously or to treat them with the authority they deserve is to force a literal read on every passage. Not so with Origen. In fact, quite the opposite: the persons who treat the Scriptures as making up a divine book allow them to guide us rather than impose our own presuppositions on it.[13]

The idea that the Scriptures contain "impossibilities" or inaccurate accounting of events may be so strange to us that a longer quotation is worth considering:

> . . . the Word of God has arranged for certain stumbling-blocks, as it were, and hindrances and impossibilities to be inserted in the midst of the law and the history, in order that we may not be completely drawn away by the sheer attractiveness of the language . . . because the principal aim was to announce the connexion that exists among spiritual events, those that have already happened and those that are yet to come to pass, whenever the Word found that things which had happened in history could

> be harmonised with these mystical events he used them, concealing from the multitude their deeper meaning. But wherever in the narrative the accomplishment of some particular deeds, which had been previously recorded for the sake of their more mystical meanings, did not correspond with the sequence of the intellectual truths, the Scriptures wove into the story something which did not happen, occasionally something which could not happen, and occasionally something which might have happened but in fact did not. Sometimes a few words are inserted which in the bodily sense are not true, and at other times a greater number . . . not only did the Spirit supervise the writings which were previous to the coming of Christ, but because he is the same Spirit and proceeds from the one God he has dealt in like manner with the gospels and the writings of the apostles. For the history even of these is not everywhere pure, events being woven together in the bodily sense without having actually happened; nor do the law and the commandments contained therein entirely declare what is reasonable.[14]

There are several points to consider. First, there can be no doubt but that Origen has a high view of the inspiration of the Scriptures. He notes, as we did at the outset, that the Holy Spirit supervised the writings of both Testaments. Earlier, we noted that he referenced the Scriptures as divine writings. So, he sees them as the product of God's direction and the final version of the Bible has the words God intended it to have. Second, coupled with this strong sense of them saying what God intended, we see an equally strong affirmation that they contain what he calls "stumbling-blocks"—nonhistorical events, for example. Again, Origen is crystal clear on this. The stumbling blocks he mentions are not the accidental additions of later copiers, but rather are there precisely because God intentionally put them there. Third, he is pretty clear on why these two claims go together. In the first place, God does not want us distracted from the deeper meaning by the sheer attractiveness of the language and stories. In the second place and more importantly, Origen seems implicitly to recognize again the importance of our "struggle" with the Scriptures. If all were evident on first read, we would become lazy, never progressing more deeply into the life of faith. This depth is only accomplished by ongoing investigation that leads to our formation and reformation through our effort to understand the deep mysteries of God. Finally, I have not yet used the word, but one of the things for which Origen is known and for which he is building a case, is what we call *allegorical interpretation*—a method of interpreting the Scriptures that believes that the point being communicated by the writers is different than the literal meaning. There are a number of interesting points about allegorical interpretation.

First, I know scholars for whom the notion of allegorical interpretation is a slippery slope that allows interpreters to twist the Bible to say anything they wish. This is a reasonable concern, as it does open the door to abuse. However, one has to wonder, what approach to biblical interpretation has been able to avoid abuse? There is one question here that matters and it is this: did God intend us to use allegory as a means to interpret the Scriptures? Origen gives us a good argument for why the answer is yes.

Second, within the church of Origen's time and for some time after, we can identify two different interpretive traditions: one known as the Antiochene school and the other as the Alexandrian school, for the location of their respective centers of scholarship. A central element of the Alexandrian school of interpretation was the acceptance of allegorical interpretation. The Antiochene school resisted allegorical interpretation. As we noted at the outset, Origen's work was centered in Alexandria. Now, what is particularly interesting is which of the schools seemed most frequently to end up with heretical doctrinal positions. During the modern period (from, say, 1600 to the late 1900s), rationalistic individualism increasingly tended toward more literal meanings of texts, with a strong preference for the "plain meaning" conveyed by the texts. So, one might expect that the looser interpretive methods of allegorical readings would be more likely to lead to error. However, precisely the opposite was true. It was the more literal typological interpretative approach of the Antiochenes that tended more often to end up in error.

Third, one might reasonably wonder why this would be the case—why did those who took the writings more literally seem more frequently to come to erroneous conclusions? One has to admit that Origen is correct that there are biblical passages that seem, to use his words, "impossible," "irrational," or "unworthy of God." A person who holds to a more literalistic interpretive approach, Origen would say, must figure out ways to cover over those "stumbling-blocks." In the process, they must defend the impossible as possible, the irrational as rational, and what is unworthy of God as being worthy of God. Such attempts at reconciliation often led to difficulty, and some of the failures resulted in positions that ran counter to the canonized doctrines of the church.

Consider, for example, Athanasius, who, in his work *Contra Arianos*, argued for the divinity of Jesus and against the position of Arius, who held that Christ was not fully divine. Once, while I was teaching a course on Christian doctrine, a student read a list of biblical proof texts defending the Arian view of Jesus. It was a long list, and at one point, another student raised his hand and asked, "Well, given these proof texts, why are we not all Arians?" In other words, this student in particular was feeling the force of the biblical passages cited by the Arians. The answer Athanasius gave was that the Arians tended to read the Scriptures woodenly and literalistically. The result of this literalism, according to Athanasius and the church as a whole, was the embrace of heresy. With Origen, Athanasius readily accepted that the Scriptures do not always mean what, on first glance, they seem to mean.

Finally, consider a well-known verse of the Scriptures from 2 Timothy 3:16:

> All scripture is inspired by God and is useful for teaching, for reproof, for correction, and for training in righteousness. (NRSV)

The Greek word that is translated as "inspired by God" here is *theopneustos*, which literally means "God-breathed." This word appears nowhere else in the Scriptures. So, we do not have other usages to fall back on to help us understand more about what it means. However, for our purposes, we need not dig too much deeper on the meaning of the term. Rather, consider one of our initial points—that the church saw writings beyond those in the official canon as important for the life of faith. In Chapter 5 we explore some writings of Basil the Great. His brother, Gregory of Nyssa, made an interesting statement about Basil's commentary on Genesis. He called it *theopneustos*—that is, Gregory considered Basil's commentary to be God-breathed.

Now, I want to be clear. The point here is not to reduce the significance of the word *theopneustos*, nor is the point to undermine the importance of the word as applied to biblical writings. Rather, I intend to resist the contemporary tendency to underemphasize the importance of other texts within the broad canonical heritage of the church for Christian life and practice. I wish to elevate their importance and, thereby, once again to draw attention to the contribution important, nonbiblical writings have made to the life of faith and the life of the church. As Ted Peters once wrote, while the early church clearly took the Scriptures to be inspired by God, it did not claim that the Scriptures were the only writings that were inspired by God. Certainly, this was explicitly the case with Gregory and his view of Basil's commentary on Genesis.

Ideas to Consider

We have gleaned a number of insights from our look into the early church period, some of which are, no doubt, surprising to our contemporary sensibilities. As we conclude this chapter, let's summarize:

1. The official books of the Old and New Testaments were settled at a relatively late date. The Holy Spirit's guidance of the growth of the early church was going on at the same time as settling the biblical books.

2. Throughout the writings of the early church fathers we see a focus on how the Scriptures relate to human salvation, to the conversion of life. The aim is not primarily to convey historical events (though that is, as Origen notes, most frequently a secondary goal), but more to form us into the image of Christ, that is, to lead us into a full-fledged conversion of life.
3. Even when the official books of the Old and New Testaments were settled, the early church recognized the importance of books beyond those officially named as canon. We learned that Athanasius, in the very same letter that named the canonical books, affirmed the importance of certain books that went beyond the canon. For the most part, these are the books that are in the Catholic Bible, but not generally in Protestant Bibles.
4. The church had a strong sense of the Spirit's attendance to the process whereby the Scriptures came into existence and became identified as the Scriptures. Origen, as we saw, clearly believed that they contain what God intended.
5. Coupled with the belief that the Scriptures contain what God intends, one of the two major strands of interpretation held that the Scriptures sometimes contain nonhistorical content. Origen builds the defense for this view.
6. The interpretive approach defended by Origen and the Alexandrian school was less likely to draw heretical accusations in its interpretation of the Bible.
7. While the early church clearly considered the Scriptures to be inspired by God, it never claimed that the Scriptures were

> the only writings inspired by God. In fact, they occasionally identified other writings as inspired by God and encouraged that they be read and seriously studied.

You may recall one of the many versions of the story of the youngster who desperately wants a pet duck. In response to the child's entreaties, the parents buy a young duck for their son. The boy is overwhelmed with joy at the gift and immediately takes it out for play. The boy loves the duck so much, he wants to hold and embrace it. However, he loves it too much and as his embrace grows tighter and tighter, the duck's breathing becomes labored and it is eventually killed. The boy is heartbroken over the loss and cannot understand how this has happened. The thing he loved so much he has strangled, precisely because he loved it so much.

Perhaps we contemporaries do this with the Scriptures. We love them so much and are so thankful to God for giving this wonderful book to us. In the process, we grasp it tightly, imposing our sense of what it means to honor and respect it upon the text. In our very attempt to "love it," we strangle the Spirit's ability to speak to us through it, because we want to "love it" on our own terms. As the parable of the duck reminds us, living things must be both loved and respected in their own right. Similarly important is the early church's willingness to let the Scriptures speak on their own terms, not insisting they conform to our presupposed notions of genre and history. In so doing, they sought to give the Spirit full freedom to use all the wide range of writing tools available (metaphor, simile, exaggeration, and so on).

As we are discovering in our study together, taking a look at the writings of the early church can often reveal how often our contemporary faith communities overlook the deep and wide riches that constitute the broader Christian tradition. The Scriptures are one example of that. Let's now turn our attention to another.

II.

Unity and Schism in the Early Church

To what extent was the body of Christ unified during the first few centuries of its history? Sometimes we are presented with an overly optimistic, perhaps mythical, view of the early church, characterized without dispute or disagreement. Of course, this myth is just that . . . a myth—and one that does not correspond to the way things actually were. The New Testament itself records disagreements between leaders. Debates with the gnostics (a group that held that *true Christian faith* was handed down via "special" or "secret" knowledge from Jesus through his followers) started very early, as did the Arian controversy (a movement that rejected a fully divine nature in Jesus). In fact, it was the early church's confidence that these other belief systems were dangerous and destructive that contributed significantly to the development of a canon of Scripture and official church doctrine. In what follows, though, I want to distinguish movements the church successfully fended off as heresy from larger institutional schisms that resulted in a fragmented body of Christ and competing traditions of faith under the broader Christian banner.

For roughly the first one thousand years of church history, there was essentially one, united church. The first major institutional split between followers of Jesus did not come until 1054 when the Eastern church and the Western church divided over a question about the relationships among Father, Son, and Holy Spirit.[1] A relatively subtle theological difference arose when the later Latin version of the Nicene Creed contained the term *filioque*, which was not in the original Greek version. After an extended period of dispute, the Eastern church divided from the Western church in objection to the term's inclusion in the creed. They believed that the term established an unacceptable hierarchy within the trinitarian persons—Father, Son, and Holy Spirit.

About five hundred years later, Luther nailed his Ninety-five Theses to the door of the Castle Church in Wittenberg, launching the Protestant Reformation. What was intended initially as a discussion between scholars led to the second major rupture in the church. In addition to *objections* to certain practices of the Roman Catholic Church, Luther also argued *for* the "priesthood of all believers." He believed that every individual had direct access to God without the need for a priest as mediator, making every person essentially his or her own priest. Closely connected was the idea that individual believers could interpret the Bible for themselves, without the mediating work of the church. While certainly not made intentionally, these moves opened the door to further divisions, eventually leading to contemporary denominationalism.

You do not have to see the Protestant Reformation as a bad thing[2] in order to see that these changes in beliefs have had both good and bad consequences. Both the move to the priesthood of all believers and the defense of every Christian's ability to interpret the Bible represented a movement in the general direction of individualism. The bonds of church authority diminished and the period after these changes saw a rapid growth in the number of different believing bodies, or denominations. Initially, Luther had taken action to correct what he saw as serious papal and clerical errors. Sadly, an unintended outcome was the release of individuals to form whatever kind of church they believed appropriate based on their own reading of the Scriptures. In correcting the centralized power of the papacy and priestly system, Luther's work also opened the door to the many, many denominations and sub-denominations we see today.

Do you realize how fractured the body of Christ is today? In the New Testament, Jesus speaks of nonbelievers being able to identify Christians by their love and unity. I wonder how those words fare in a world with so many different kinds of Christians. Do you know the number of different Christian denominations? The number runs into five figures, with higher estimates running in excess of thirty thousand different denominations and sub-denominations.[3] In other words, the church that Jesus said would be characterized by love and unity has now fractured to the point that, frankly, we do not look united at all. With up to thirty thousand different identifiable Christian denominations, can we even consider using the term *unity*? The early church was quite willing to exclude those who were not able to make the appropriate doctrinal affirmations, but that was a move to keep church unity by expelling those who would upset that unity. And, it is critically important to note that they saved this move for only a handful of what they took to be critical doctrines. What they were not willing to do, for the entirety of the first millennium, was allow disagreements to result in multiple independent church bodies and hierarchies. The images they used to describe the effects of allowing divisions within the body of Christ were often graphic. Images of "rending the body of Christ" or severing body parts from our Lord by virtue of schism were common. In what follows, we consider some of those statements and see what insights we, as contemporary readers, might find.

As I noted at the outset, there were many challenges to Christian faith, even during the earliest period of church history. Different groups, espousing competing doctrines on numerous important points, seemed perpetually to disrupt the faith. The church foresaw the anarchy that would follow laxity around important doctrines and the question of ecclesial authority. So it responded aggressively to what it perceived as heretical teaching and the corresponding threat of schism.

Let us turn to one of the more serious heretical threats of the early period, gnosticism, and to one of the strongest respondents. It was the early church father whose name means "peace": St. Irenaeus, Bishop of Lyon. He was born in the first half of the second century (with the exact date uncertain) to Christian parents. Irenaeus was said to have studied at the feet of Polycarp (a martyr for the faith), who in turn was a disciple of the Apostle John. Irenaeus escaped the persecution at Lyon instigated by Marcus Aurelius, having been sent to Rome to weigh in on the heretical teachings of Montanus. When he returned to Lyon, he found that the bishop had been martyred. Subsequently, Irenaeus was named the second bishop of Lyon. It was during this period (ca. A.D. 190) that he wrote his response to gnosticism, known simply as *Against Heresies.* Against accepted church teaching, the gnostics argued that there was an unbroken tradition of "secret knowledge" dating all the way back to Jesus. It was in this "secret knowledge" that humans were to find salvation and right relationship with God. Irenaeus recognized the inherent threats of heresy and the attendant schism, and his arguments for Christian unity were simple and straightforward.

First, he pointed out that all Christian bishops were clearly identifiable, all the way back to the apostles, and none had been gnostics. Second, he noted the importance of embracing unity in doctrinal authority (based on tradition and the Scriptures). He went on to say that the councils and the bishop of Rome constituted that doctrinal authority. As we have noted before, there are some matters on which the church councils did not take a position. One might reasonably hold differing positions on these matters. However, Irenaeus was both straightforward and clear: when the church as a whole, through the conciliar process, canonized a particular doctrine, Christians everywhere were to embrace it. This work still stands as a major contribution to the life of the church. Some traditions hold that Irenaeus was martyred, but most consider this unlikely, and he died in 202.

Let's take a look at *Against Heresies* to see how Irenaeus phrased his defense of Christian unity:

> As I have already observed, the Church, having received this preaching and this faith, although scattered throughout the whole world, yet, as if occupying but one house, carefully preserves it. She also believes these points [of doctrine] just as if she had but one soul, and one and the same heart, and she proclaims them, and teaches them, and hands them down, with perfect harmony, as if she possessed only one mouth. For, although the languages of the world are dissimilar, yet the import of the tradition is one and the same. For the Churches which have been planted in Germany do not believe or hand down anything different, nor do those in Spain, nor those in Gaul, nor those in the East, nor those in Egypt, nor those in Libya, nor those which have been established in the central regions of the world. But as the sun, that creature of God, is one and the same throughout the whole world, so also the preaching of the truth shineth everywhere, and enlightens all men that are willing to come to knowledge of the truth. Nor will any one of the rulers in the Churches, however gifted he may be in point of eloquence, teach doctrines different from these (for no one is greater than the Master); nor, on the other hand, will he who is deficient in power of expression inflict injury on the tradition. For the faith being ever one and the same, neither does one who is able at great length to discourse regarding it, make any addition to it, nor does one, who can say but little, diminish it.[4]

In the preceding section, Irenaeus had laid out what he took to be the foundations of Christian faith. While the creeds of Nicea and Constantinople where still over a century away, his statement of the faith was along the same lines—trinitarian, Christ-centered, and focused on human salvation. His argument for unity is implicitly connected to God's revelation in the life and teachings of Jesus. Explicitly, he argues that the Christian faith has been one from the beginning, throughout the world wherever Christian faith is practiced and observed. As he notes, the same truth proclaimed everywhere "shineth" to "enlighten" any willing to hear the truth. After his defense of Christian unity, he moves directly to address the problems with gnostic claims, focusing on where they depart from the received teaching.

Consistent with his strong sense of the importance of Christian unity, Irenaeus has harsh words for those who would create schism among the followers of Jesus:

> He shall judge also those who give rise to schisms, who are destitute of the love of God, and who look to their own special advantage rather than to the unity of the Church; and who for trifling reasons, or any kind of reason which occurs to them, cut in pieces and divide the great and glorious body of Christ, and so far as in them lies [positively] destroy it,—men who prate of peace while they give rise to war, and do in truth strain out a gnat, but swallow a camel. For no reformation of so great importance can be effected by them, as will compensate for the mischief arising from their schism. He shall also judge all those who are beyond the pale of the truth, that is, who are outside the Church; but he himself shall be judged by no one. For to him all things are consistent: he has a full faith in one God Almighty, of whom are all things; and in the Son of God, Jesus Christ our Lord, by whom are all things, and in the dispensations connected with Him, by means of which the Son of God became man; and a firm belief in the Spirit of God, who furnishes us with a knowledge of the truth, and has set forth the dispensations of the Father and the Son, in virtue of which He dwells with every generation of men, according to the will of the Father.[5]

It is noteworthy that Irenaeus recognizes that a good many schisms are the result of "trifling" pursuit of self-interest. What might count as a "trifling" reason for division? Perhaps dividing from Christian brothers and sisters over the style of music we prefer, or the kinds of instruments we allow to accompany our music? What about differences of opinion over worship orders? Would it be trifling to divide over the frequency with which we partake of Holy Communion? Or, what about heading off to start a new church over our preference for a different version of the Bible than our current church uses? All of these and even more trifling reasons have resulted in divisions among those who name Jesus as their Lord. Irenaeus was prescient of our contemporary times. He makes it clear that, in his view, trifling reasons can never justify "the mischief arising from [the] schism."

It is not surprising that in the later part of the quotation, Irenaeus picks up on those who would divide the body of Christ over heretical doctrine. He summarizes again the common Christian faith and simply observes that those who would embrace another doctrine are "outside the Church."[6] He does not conclude that those who believe a different doctrine ought to establish their own church, rather he matter-of-factly observes that they are not part of the church. Since they are not a part of the church, their departure cannot lead to schism. In our contemporary, postmodern world, I suspect that this solution to the question of what constitutes right doctrine sounds a bit "oppressive" and "centralized." This is perhaps an overreaction. The two poles that are rightly resisted are "everyone believes what they choose" over against "one person decides right doctrine." In fact, the early church suggested neither, but rather put their confidence in the Holy Spirit's guidance of a conciliar process. This process brought together church leaders and scholars from all over and set them at a table together to jointly, with prayer and discernment, work out official church doctrine. Many different voices and perspectives came together and discussions were often long and nuanced. At the end, any solution to the right doctrine question involves a decision of where to place one's faith. In this case, the church opted for a process that invited communal discernment with the direct invocation of the Holy Spirit's guidance. It is hard to imagine a better process, given the options open to us.

Before moving on from Irenaeus, one last point deserves attention. Notice the metaphors he uses to describe the effect of schism on the church:

> . . . and who for trifling reasons, or any kind of reason which occurs to them, cut in pieces and divide the great and glorious body of Christ, and so far as in them lies [positively] destroy it. . . .

He compares schism in the church with cutting into pieces the body of Christ. And the longer-term outcome, if schism is allowed to continue? If it were possible, it would lead to the destruction of the body of Christ. This is a metaphor we will find repeated in others of the early church fathers, and it is a very sobering one indeed.

Consider Clement of Rome. In this short quotation from his letter to the Corinthians, he captures Irenaeus's point about unity built around belief in one and the same God and Lord Jesus. In addition, we see him using the same images to describe schism—the image of rending the body of Christ:

> Why are there quarrels and ill will and dissensions and schism and fighting among you? Do we not have one God and one Christ, and one Spirit of grace poured out upon us? And is there not one calling in Christ? Why do we wrench and tear apart the members of Christ, and revolt against our own body, and reach such folly as to forget that we are members of one another?[7]

Our "one calling" to faith ought to overcome the natural human tendency toward self-centeredness, Clement says. Then, he puts the strongest point on the damage caused by schism. He tells us that when we divide from each other, those of us united in Christ, we are effectively damaging "our own body." How so? The body of Christ into which we have been engrafted is damaged, and thus, to embrace schism is to damage ourselves.

More than a century after Irenaeus, Hilary of Poitiers would write against heresy as well. He, like Clement of Rome and Irenaeus before him, focused on the unity of the church, based primarily on the unity of what the church taught. In addressing what gives rise to heresy, Hilary observes that it happens when persons, rather than bending their own understanding to the Scriptures, bend the Scriptures to their own ends:

> But I trust that the Church, by the light of her doctrine, will so enlighten the world's vain wisdom, that, even though it accept not the mystery of the faith, it will recognise that in our conflict with heretics we, and not they, are the true representatives of that mystery. . . . It is obvious that these dissensions concerning the faith result from a distorted mind, which twists the words of Scripture into conformity with its opinion, instead of adjusting that opinion to the words of Scripture.[8]

Of course, as we noted in the earlier chapter on the Scriptures, many persons come to different interpretations of the same biblical passages. How did the fathers say we were to avoid error in our interpretation? They were largely in agreement on the answer: the correct interpretation of Scripture is given by the Holy Spirit, working through the church as a whole, and not through one person. Whenever one's own interpretation runs counter to that given by the church, one must submit to the teaching of the church, rather than following his or her interpretation. Submission to the dual authority of Scripture and the church was central to the fathers' understanding of Christian authority and that, in turn, was central to how one avoids "opinions" that lead to schism.

Cyprian of Carthage writes of the authority that abides in the leader of the church, taking a more explicitly Roman Catholic position on authority:

> For this has been the source from which heresies and schism have arisen, that God's priest is not obeyed, nor do people reflect that there is for the time one priest in the Church, who for the time is judge instead of Christ, and if the whole brotherhood would obey him, according to divine teaching, no one would stir up anything against the college of priests. . . .[9]

Cyprian implicitly has in mind Jesus' selection of Peter as the leader of the church after his ascension. After Christ departed, he knew questions of interpretation would arise and decisions would have to be made on a whole host of ecclesial and doctrinal matters. In selecting Peter, Christ centered decision making in one person, one priest, for the church, so goes the claim. What causes heresy and the subsequent schisms and divisions in the church? Cyprian says these problems arise because there are those in the church who refuse to submit themselves to the authority of the appointed leader. In time, of course, this gave way to the conciliar approach mentioned above. It is, as we noted, a very Roman Catholic answer to the question. At the same time, it is hard not to agree that heresy, schism, and division often arise because church members are unwilling to submit themselves to the authority of the church, even on relatively inconsequential matters. In our contemporary Western world, where individual liberty is the greatest of all virtues, submission to the authority of the church seems anachronistic to us.

In another letter, Cyprian writes to individuals who have separated from the church and established another, set up with a different bishop:

> For it weighs me down and saddens me, and the intolerable grief of a smitten, almost prostrate, spirit seizes me, when I find that you there, contrary to ecclesiastical order, contrary to evangelical law, contrary to the unity of the Catholic institution, had consented that another bishop should be made. That is what is neither right nor allowable to be done; that another church should be set up; that Christ's members should be torn asunder; that the one mind and body of the Lord's flock should be lacerated by a divided emulation.[10]

In an age where it is easy to start a church outside any ecclesiastical authorities, it surely sounds strange, the concern Cyprian expresses over division. Once again, we see the characterization of church division as ripping apart the body of Christ. When faced with the choice between allowing church division and martyrdom,

Dionysius argued that it was better to die than to allow the body of Christ to be damaged by division:

> For it would have been but dutiful to have suffered any kind of ill, so as to avoid rending the Church of God. And a martyrdom borne for the sake of preventing a division of the Church, would not have been more inglorious than one endured for refusing to worship idols; nay, in my opinion at least, the former would have been a nobler thing than the latter. For in the one case a person gives such a testimony simply for his own individual soul, whereas in the other case he is a witness for the whole Church.[11]

In a later chapter, we examine cases where early Christians were willing to be martyred rather than participate in the worship of idols. In particular, we consider the willingness to die rather than to perform certain rituals in honor of the emperor. Here, Dionysius compares the two, saying it is even better to die for the unity of the church than to die for resisting idolatry. Why? In the latter case, the resister is martyred for his or her own faith; but in the former, the sacrifice is on behalf of the whole church. The potential is for the salvation of all those impacted by the schism, and thus the martyr dies to preserve all those souls.

In a final quotation, rather than speaking of the negative impacts of allowing church division, our good friend, John Chrysostom, simply affirms the importance of the church:

> Secede not from the Church: for nothing is stronger than the Church. Thy hope is the Church; thy salvation is the Church; thy refuge is the Church. It is higher than the heavens and wider than the earth. It never grows old, but

> is ever full of vigor. Wherefore Holy Writ pointing to its strength and stability calls it a mountain.[12]

When we read the word *church* in this and other passages like it, I suspect we simply think of our own church. If we are members of any one of the thirty thousand plus denominations in the world today, we see ourselves referenced in this and other passages like it. This was not what Chrysostom would have had in mind, however. No, he would have been thinking much more narrowly. The church to him was one, under one system of leadership, affirming the same doctrine, and united across ethnic and geographical lines. In his affirmation of the one church, Chrysostom suggests the words of our Lord when he established the church. He knew what we have observed before: the hope of the world is Jesus, and God has chosen the church to be the way that the good news of Jesus is spread throughout the world. Let me say again, one need not put the denominational genie back in the bottle to agree that the fragmentation of the church is largely for "trifling" reasons and constitutes a weak witness to what Christ intended the church to be.

Practically, what might we do about all this? Given where we are with denominational fragmentation and the rise of independent, Congregationalist churches, we are not likely to see large-scale or even modest moves toward reunifying the splintered church. Once splintered, divided factions can reunite, but it is rarely the case that it happens. The taste of independence, the ability to "make our own decisions," and the right to exercise "religious freedom"—even if it means substantially changing Christian doctrine—are all too deeply embedded in our way of thinking to expect significant change. Add to this what we examine in Chapter 4 about living in a culture that so treasures individual liberty—the right to do and worship as one pleases—and the likelihood of meaningful reunification, across or within denominational lines, is very slim.

I have suggestions to help heal some of the fragmentation, but I am worried that we are so fragmented that even these modest proposals are going to sound extreme. First, we all serve the same Lord and Christ. It was our Lord who established Holy Communion. Would it not seem reasonable that, across denominational boundaries, we might be able to share Holy Communion together, recognizing that it is God's meal to which we invite one another and not our own? We call on all participants to examine their own soul to ensure that they are ready to partake. Do we have to add a layer of our own approval? Do we have to take possession of the meal in such a way that we can only share it with those who believe exactly as we do? We must look pretty childish to the outside world when we cannot even agree to sit and eat together in the one sacrament we all agree was instituted by our Lord. All the many strands of Protestantism, Catholicism, and Eastern Orthodoxy are bound together by agreement on the overwhelming majority of Christian belief and practice. Let us move past the relatively smaller areas of disagreement and welcome one another to the Lord's Table. Let us model for the world, in this one event, the unity Christ had in mind for us.

Second, our baptism is a work of God, not a human work. By that, I mean when a person is baptized, it is God's Spirit who does the work of marking and engrafting the baptized into the body of Christ. Do we not insult the work of the Holy Spirit when we think a person has to be baptized again if they join "our" denomination? Do we think that, somehow, that "other" denomination is so perverse that the very Spirit of God could not fulfill his role in the baptism? Some denominations hold that a person must be immersed in the baptismal waters; others sprinkle, and yet others pour. However, the early church took no official position on how baptism was to be performed. It did not insist that, unless done in one and only one of those three ways, the baptism was not valid. There are records of all three methods. Is it not time to welcome Christians from other churches into ours without the embarrassing notion that they have to be baptized all over again? "Alien baptism"? Really? That we even have such a term is an indicator of how badly our theology suffers from ignorance of the broader Christian tradition.

Third, as I noted above, by and large, with the only exceptions being some far-out sects or cults, Christians agree on far more points of doctrine and practice than they disagree on. Given that fact, would it not seem reasonable to treat each other with a bit more respect? There is an old joke that tells about two men meeting at a conference. In the course of discussion, one notes that he is a Christian. Much to his delight, the other man smiles broadly and indicates he, too, is a follower of Jesus. This emboldens the man, who goes on to say he is a member of the Church of God. Again, the second man smiles, nodding and indicating that he is also a member of that church. The first man, feeling very good now, goes on to indicate the sub-tradition of the Church of God, when he says, "I am a member of the Church of God—Anderson." Once more, the second man indicates he is as well. Finally, the first man, ready to lay all the cards on the table, says, "I am a member of the Church of God—Anderson, New Constitution." The second man looks aghast and shouts, "Die, heretic! I'm Church of God—Anderson, Old Constitution."[13]

Funny? Of course, at some level; but it is all too real when it comes to reminding us of the "trifling" matters that divide us. And, not just divide us, but lead us to consider those who disagree with us to be heretics. This should stop, immediately. We need to get to the point where we can welcome those of other sub-traditions as the Christian brothers and sisters that they are and stop unhelpful recriminations and criticisms.

Finally, consider the pastor of a United Methodist congregation in Indiana. While he is a committed Wesleyan, theologically, he has a remarkable ability to learn from those who think differently than he does. Once appointed to his church, he wasted little time in forming a group of pastors, all from different traditions. Each week, they met together, prayed together, and discussed passages they would be preaching from that week. Their perspectives were different, and they sometimes came to rather different conclusions about the passages they discussed. However, the group stayed together and met regularly over an extended time because they each found the fellowship delightful. Even when they disagreed, they found one another's perspective helpful in better understanding the rich Christian tradition.

We need more pastors taking initiatives like this, bridging gaps and uniting across traditional and sub-traditional boundaries whenever possible. As I recall, this group eventually had the courage to invite one another as guest speakers/preachers on special occasions. Imagine that: not only enriching themselves through their times of fellowship, but also bringing their congregations into the conversation. And, in the process, they, at least for a while, closed the gap between the differing denominations.

I encourage you to think of other ways to bridge the gap between Christian brothers and sisters in different denominations and traditions. Take down the walls that separate us, give those who believe differently on "trifling" matters the space to be different. And, above all, remember that our Lord once said that those outside the church would recognize those who were his followers by virtue of our love for one another and our unity around his Lordship!

III.

Discipleship in the Early Church

The overwhelming majority of my church experience has been within the broader Protestant tradition. I am a United Methodist, grew up in the Southern Baptist church, and have attended a number of other denominations within Protestantism—including several versions of Presbyterianism, and churches in the Episcopal, Disciples of Christ, and Lutheran denominations. I have attended a Roman Catholic church from time to time and have enjoyed several visits to a Trappist monastery in Kentucky. However, when it comes to the question of what it means to become a part of a local body of Christ, all of my experiences are within Protestantism, mostly in the United Methodist and the Southern Baptist churches.

What is required for someone to become a participant, or even a member, of a particular church within a given a denomination or tradition? When I was a youngster, in a Southern Baptist church, if you wanted to join the church, the requirements were simple and straightforward. If you were not a Christian, you accepted Christ, often by a trip forward during an altar call. The pastor would ask some basic questions that allowed you to make a public profession of your newfound faith. Once that was done, the congregation would vote to accept you as a new member. On the first opportunity, you would be baptized, finalizing the process. As I recall, there was no training or educational steps that I had to traverse before I could be baptized. In those traditions where there is a doctrinal commitment to baptismal regeneration, new converts are often baptized immediately upon profession of faith. While what I have described above was my experience, it is certainly possible that other Southern Baptist churches had more complex rituals for accepting and initiating a new follower of Jesus into their fellowship.

In The United Methodist Church, the *Book of Worship* has a formal series of questions and answers that are exchanged between the pastor and the one seeking first conversion and then, membership. This simple ritual offers a "low threshold" set of expectations and requirements from those who would join themselves to the body of Christ.

So, other than a ritual of conversion and a ritual for joining the church (initially, and then, any time a membership is transferred from one church to another), what is required to become part of a church? Generally, the answer is nothing. In fact, many churches in our contemporary context are so happy to have someone indicate a desire to join that requirements are usually kept to a bare minimum. After all, if one church requires too much, the potential member might simply decide to join one with less stringent requirements. Now, there are some churches who name expectations for anyone wishing to become a member, and they take these expectations quite seriously. I do not want to paint a picture that is entirely "laissez faire" when it comes to church participation today. At the same time, the majority of churches resist identifying requirements or expectations of those who would join our local congregations. It is a consumer culture, after all, right? And, one has to cater to the consumer. So, we must keep the barriers to participation low, allow folks to come and go, moving from one congregation to another without resistance, and focus our marketing on what "we" have that "they" do not.

At this point I want to make clear an intentional shift from talking about the constellation of issues around joining the church/church membership/church participation on the one hand to talking about discipleship and catechesis. The two topics are much more closely aligned than they often seem to be in our contemporary churches. And, the early church in particular saw training in discipleship (catechesis) as a critical part of bringing a person into the faith. In what follows, I will likely dart back and forth across the line, sometimes talking more in membership terms and other times talking more in discipleship terms. The goal is to help us learn from the early church about the importance of making sure we equip new Christians so that they may successfully live out the life of faith.

This laissez faire attitude toward participation in the life of the church was not always the case. In an essay called "Early Church Catechesis," Clinton Arnold notes some differences between our attitudes and those of the early church:

> I had also been doing some reading in the Church fathers about how new Christians' classes were conducted in the early church and came away deeply convicted about the superficiality of what we were doing. There was such a rigorous plan and

> commitment by church leaders in the first four centuries to ground new believers in their Christian lives. . . .
>
> These new people clearly have some rudimentary level of faith. They appear to be aware of enough of the gospel message that they have exercised faith in it and are now taking the step to commit themselves to a rigorous course of study, prepare for baptism, and join the community of believers. In the language of contemporary conversionist evangelicalism, one might say that they have heard an evangelistic message, prayed the sinner's prayer, and are ready to get plugged into a church.
>
> The difficulty, however, is that the catechumenate was also a formal preparation for baptism. Perhaps the most significant motive for the shift away from the apostolic practice of baptizing immediately after profession of faith to a time after substantive training, mentoring, and preparation had to do with "the concern the ministers of baptism had from the very beginning for the sincerity of the conversion of the candidates."[1]

In the early church period, there was less concern for church marketing, and as Arnold notes, much more concern for a conversion that led to transformation into a life of discipleship. The church did not feel it had to compete with others because it believed that it held the oracles of life and the only avenue to relationship with God. In other words, the church did not feel it had to "sell itself" because it had been empowered by its Lord to be the agent of reconciliation—between humans and God and between humans. What they had, everyone needed, and they took these inherent responsibilities with profound seriousness, often in the form of a prolonged period of teaching or "catechesis."

Gregory of Nyssa, who with his brother Basil the Great and another Gregory, Gregory of Nazianzus, made up the three early theologians known as the Cappadocian fathers. These three were the most influential in forming the church's language describing the trinitarian nature of God. Gregory of Nyssa, arguably, made the largest contribution to the final form of the doctrine as embodied in the Creed of Constantinople of 381. Gregory, sometimes called Nyssa for simplicity, was born in 335 and was Basil's younger brother. In our discussions about wealth and poverty in Chapter 5, we will meet the family of Basil and Gregory. It is an interesting side note of church history that Gregory was named after another Gregory, Gregory Thaumaturgus (that is, Gregory the Wonderworker). While Basil was the better administrator, Gregory was the brilliant theologian. The Neo-Platonism of Plotinus was a major influence on Gregory's thinking, and it undoubtedly contributed to his articulation of key Christian doctrines, particularly, as noted above, the doctrine of the Trinity. While not entirely happy with taking on the responsibility, Gregory became Bishop of Nyssa when appointed by Basil. Gregory died in 395.

Two of Gregory of Nyssa's greatest contributions to Christian theology were his work on the doctrine of the Trinity and his exploration of God's infinite nature. At the same time, though, Gregory wrote important works on the life of faith. His *Life of Moses* used the stages of Moses' life as metaphors for our growth in Christian faith. Gregory also focused on the importance of catechesis, or training in the faith. His *Catechetical Oration* was written to serve as a guide to teachers preparing persons for baptism. It states the faith in a way intended to both educate and respond to potential objections.

James Herbert Strawley, in his 1903 classic presentation of the *Catechetical Oration*, identifies a four-part outline:

I. Chapters 1–4 in which he expounds the doctrine of the Trinity.

II. Chapters 5–8 in which he treats the creation of man and the origin of evil.

III. Chapters 9–32, which deal at length with the Incarnation, removing objections, and showing its consistency with the moral attributes of God. In the same section Gregory treats the method of Atonement.

IV. Chapters 33–40, which treat of the sacraments of baptism and the Eucharist, and the moral conditions (faith and repentance) necessary for their right use.[2]

Remember that Gregory's work is intended to serve as a guide to those engaged in teaching folks new in the faith. It provides an overview of the Christian faith that begins with the nature of God, focusing on the uniquely Christian doctrine of the Trinity, then moves to the doctrine of creation and humanity, with particular attention to human sin. After identifying the human predicament, Gregory describes the solution that God undertakes to resolve the problem. The third section, dealing with the Incarnation of the Eternal Son and the doctrine of Atonement, is understandably the longest of the book. Finally, he moves to the sacraments that constitute a critical part of the Christian life, addressing first baptism, the mark of entry into the community, and then Holy Communion, the centerpiece of the fellowship of the church. While not a systematic theology, he offers an excellent starting point for new Christians who likely knew little about Christian faith. Now, remember, this catechetical training was not intended to *follow baptism*, but rather was to be undertaken as one prepared for baptism.

In the prologue, Gregory gives an overview of his rationale for why a serious period of catechetical instruction is important, and he summarizes how he sees the approach that might be taken.

> The presiding ministers of the "mystery of godliness" have need of a system in their instructions, in order that the Church might be replenished by the accession of such as should be saved, through the teaching of the word of Faith being brought home to the hearing of unbelievers. Not that the same method of instruction will be suitable in the case of all who approach the word. The catechism must be adapted to the diversities of their religious worship; with an eye, indeed, to the one aim and end of the system, but not using the same method of preparation in each individual case. [Gregory then discusses different types of belief systems the instructor might experience in converts.] . . . It is necessary, as I have said, to regard the opinions which the persons have taken up, and to frame your argument in accordance with the error into which each has fallen, by advancing in each discussion certain principles and reasonable propositions, that thus, through what is agreed upon on both sides, the truth may conclusively be brought to light.[3]

The church is in constant need of "replenishment" through bringing along those being saved by a period of intentional instruction. As we will see, there were times that the period of instruction, from initial indication of the desire to become a Christian until baptism, was as long as three years. Notice that Gregory does not suggest a "one size fits all" method, but rather guides the potential instructor to vary the method based on the background of the convert. In the part I omitted, he names several different religious backgrounds (Jewish, Greek, and so on) and discusses briefly how one might approach each. Likewise, because he is also very concerned about doctrinal error and heresy, he names several contemporary heresies, recognizing the root error of each. In this way, then, he sets up the rest of his work that covers the basics of teaching the Christian faith along the outline we noted above.

A contemporary of Gregory of Nyssa, Cyril of Jerusalem, is known for his catechetical series, often referenced simply as the *Catechetical Lectures.* There are a total of twenty-three, with the first eighteen aimed to instruct the new convert in the Christian faith prior to baptism. The final five, called the *mystagogical* lectures, were to be delivered to the new converts just after their baptism. They cover such matters as the sacraments of baptism, Holy Communion, and confirmation. The lectures are delivered in a pastoral tone and are replete with biblical references. Hear how Cyril wrote of the purpose of the series of lectures in the introduction:

> Study our teachings and keep them forever. Think not that they are the ordinary homilies; for though they also are good and trustworthy, yet if we should neglect them to-day we may study them to-morrow. But if the teaching concerning the layer of regeneration delivered in a consecutive course be neglected today, when shall it be made right? Suppose it is the season for planting trees: if we do not dig, and dig deep, when else can that be planted

> rightly which has once been planted ill? Suppose, pray, that the Catechising is a kind of building: if we do not bind the house together by regular bonds in the building, lest some gap be found, and the building become unsound, even our former labour is of no use. But stone must follow stone by course, and corner match with corner, and by our smoothing off inequalities the building must thus rise evenly. In like manner we are bringing to thee stones, as it were, of knowledge. Thou must hear concerning the living God, thou must hear of Judgment, must hear of Christ, and of the Resurrection. And many things there are to be discussed in succession, which though now dropped one by one are afterwards to be presented in harmonious connection. But unless thou fit them together in the one whole, and remember what is first, and what is second, the builder may build, but thou wilt find the building unsound.[4]

There are teachings and then there are *teachings*, Cyril claims, and these catechetical teachings are the latter—teachings that are always beneficial and always worth studying to deepen our faith. He cautions, however, against putting off taking full advantage of catechesis at the beginning of the life of faith. Why? Because, he says, the beginning of the life of faith is the right and proper place for catechetical instruction. Just as there is a season for planting and just as there are proper materials to use in building at different junctures, so the instruction given to those new in the faith is critical for an enduring life of discipleship. It is worth noting Cyril uses a format that, from lectures 6 through 18, follows the creed to explain the Christian faith to the new believers.

Consider one more, this from the work of St. Augustine. Around the year 406, Augustine wrote his work *On Catechising the*

Uninstructed in response to a request he received from Carthage. He begins with a response:

> You have requested me, brother Deogratias, to send you in writing something which might be of service to you in the matter of catechising the uninstructed. For you have informed me that in Carthage, where you hold the position of a deacon, persons, who have to be taught the Christian faith from its very rudiments, are frequently brought to you by reason of your enjoying the reputation of possessing a rich gift in catechising, due at once to an intimate acquaintance with the faith, and to an attractive method of discourse; but that you almost always find yourself in a difficulty as to the manner in which a suitable declaration is to be made of the precise doctrine, the belief of which constitutes us Christians: regarding the point at which our statement of the same ought to commence, and the limit to which it should be allowed to proceed: and with respect to the question whether, when our narration is concluded, we ought to make use of any kind of exhortation, or simply specify those precepts in the observance of which the person to whom we are discoursing may know the Christian life and profession to be maintained. At the same time, you have made the confession and complaint that it has often befallen you that in the course of a lengthened and languid address you have become profitless and distasteful even to yourself, not to speak of the learner whom you have been endeavoring to instruct by your utterance, and the other parties who have been present as hearers; and that you have been constrained by these straits to put upon me the constraint of that love which I owe to you, so that I may not feel it a burdensome thing among all my engagements to write you something on this subject.[5]

We learn a great deal from this short passage. First, the deacon at Carthage indicates to Augustine that the role of catechesis of those new in the faith often falls to him. The deacon understands the life of faith and its beliefs well, but he expresses concern about the form of the presentation. Where should one start? What constitute the essentials of the faith, those points critical to include in the instruction? Should it include "narration," what we might call an overview of the story of the Scriptures? Should the form be lecture and instruction? Or should it include exhortation? Finally, Augustine's inquirer confesses that, sometimes, the presentation grows long and tedious. How does one avoid boring those participating, or worse, avoid becoming bored as you present? In what follows, Augustine takes on each of these questions.

The entire outline of Augustine's course of catechesis would be worthy of our attention, but let's consider a few sections to get a sense of his response and recommendations. In true pastoral fashion, he begins with a word of encouragement for the deacon, who has expressed concern about making a boring presentation. The second section begins:

> But as regards the idea thus privately entertained by yourself in such efforts, I would not have you to be disturbed by the consideration that you have often appeared to yourself to be delivering a poor and wearisome discourse. For it may very well be the case that the matter has not so presented itself to the person whom you were trying to instruct, but that what you were uttering seemed to you to be unworthy of the ears of others, simply because it was your own earnest desire that there should be something better to listen to. Indeed with me, too, it is almost always the fact that my speech displeases myself.[6]

Sometimes, when we make a presentation to others, Augustine says, it may seem "poor and wearisome" to us—have we not all felt that way at times? This is a good thing because the feeling derives from our wishing we had an even more effective presentation. Further, he personalizes and empathizes by noting he often feels this way about his own work. Just because we have some self-doubt, however, does not mean that the presentation is not reaching its goal.

In section three, Augustine provides an initial answer to the question about narration. He says it should start with "In the beginning God created . . ." and should continue through to the present day. In other words, it should provide the catechumen an overview of the sweep of God's interaction with his world. In particular, Augustine says, attention should be focused on Jesus—the expectation for his coming from long ago; his coming in the flesh along with his life, death, and resurrection; and the statements of faith the church has developed about him.

After reminding us, in section four, that the whole reason for Christ's coming was God's great love for his human creatures, Augustine turns attention to examination of the catechumen himself or herself. The issue is straightforward—does the potential believer, when examined, give evidence of good reasons for coming to belief? Or,

> Now if he has come with a false heart, desirous only of human advantages or thinking to escape disadvantages, he will certainly speak what is untrue. Nevertheless, the very untruth which he utters should be made the point from which we start.[7]

Again in pastoral fashion, Augustine cautions against presuming that one comes from false motives, but rather encourages his friend, the deacon, to be prepared for these occurrences. When they happen, he goes on to say, the improper motives should be brought gently to the surface so that the person might still be brought to faith.

The next two sections provide an overview of the beginning of the "narration" and what should be emphasized following. The two sections after that provide insights on how to work with those who have different backgrounds. In this, he imitates Cyril's concern that the method of catechizing be undertaken in a manner most likely to be effective with the particular convert at hand. Then, in sections ten through fourteen, Augustine takes very seriously the issue raised by the deacon—how to make sure the catechumen does not become "wearied" with the presentation. Augustine names several different "sources of weariness" and coaches the deacon on how to deal with them. It is noteworthy that Augustine spends so much time on tending to the "hearer friendliness" of the presentation. For the most part, from that point on, Augustine gets into the specifics of the desired content of the catechesis through section twenty-five, which deals with "constancy of faith in the resurrection." One might say that Augustine exhorts our good deacon to "keep his eyes on the prize"—not allowing his faith to be challenged by devils, but rather remaining confident in God's power to bring all to a new creation.

After the training is complete, the catechumen is to go through a ritual and then be welcomed to his or her first Holy Communion. As Augustine puts it:

> At the conclusion of this address the person is to be asked whether he believes these things and earnestly desires to observe them. And on his replying to that effect then certainly he is to be solemnly signed and dealt with in accordance with the custom of the Church. On the subject of the sacrament, indeed, which he receives, it is first to be well impressed upon his notice that the signs of divine things are, it is true, things visible, but that the invisible things themselves are also honored in them, and that that species, which is then sanctified by the blessing, is therefore not to be regarded merely in the way in which it is regarded in any common use.[8]

The new believers make an affirmation that they believe what they have been taught in the course of catechesis and then they are "to be signed." By this, Augustine means the sign of the cross should be made over the new believers, signifying the solemnity of the event. From there, the newest church members go to participate in their first Lord's Supper; but even here, they are to be reminded that the visible signs (the bread and the wine) represent invisible, divine things. Interestingly, in the next paragraph of this section, Augustine tells the deacon that, if the presentation he has offered seems too long, he should feel free to shorten it somewhat. However, Augustine notes, it should be *no longer* than what he has written. Even at the end, Augustine worries to balance content with length, wanting to be sure the balance is appropriate.

If there is any period of instruction for new converts in our churches today, it tends to be quite short, on the order of a few weeks at most. However, it was not unusual to find periods of catechesis that extended for as long as three years. Consider these words from the *Apostolic Teaching:*

> Let him who is a catechumen be a catechumen for three years; but if any one be diligent, and has good-will to his business, let him be admitted: for it is not the length of time, but the course of life, that is judged.[9]

As we can see, the three-year period was not hard and fast, but we might ask ourselves two questions. First, how many today would be willing to submit themselves to such a regimen of study before being allowed to become a member of the body of Christ? Second, if our answer is "not many," and from that we draw the conclusion that serious catechesis is not possible in our contemporary context, what does that say about the inherent weaknesses we are building into our churches?

Different chapters of this book draw conclusions of varying degrees of strength. This chapter's study suggests a bolder conclusion. The general condition of the contemporary church is very disturbing. Our overall knowledge of the biblical narratives themselves is quite poor. When it comes to our understanding of what the early church would have considered "basic Christian doctrine," the assessment would almost certainly be even worse. The question is: what ought we to do about it? The answer lies in a return to basic catechetical instruction: maybe not the three-year course of study common for a period of the early church, but rather time enough for serious engagement in the basics of the faith.

I have used the word *catechesis* throughout because this is the term utilized by the early church to name the preparation and training in the essential elements of Christian faith. Perhaps that word sounds too academic or antiquated for us today. Yet, what we desperately need in the church is a means for providing training in both the beliefs and practices that constitute the life of faith. By taking this critical step, we offer invaluable resources, both to new converts and to those growing up in the church, that will help engender and empower living a life of discipleship. A successful program of catechesis/training in the Christian faith would have three primary components, each with important constituent parts.

First, our churches need to ensure that training is provided for all ages as part of the ongoing deepening of faith and practice. "Sunday school" can provide the weekly opportunity for meeting, though studies show that attendance at these weekly sessions is in decline. It will require a good deal of effort, I expect, to recapture our members' attention, given our general laissez-faire attitude toward Sunday morning worship attendance. Or, we may have to consider alternative times such as focused periods of intense training rather than the traditional weekly meetings. In addition to a program of training and education for those already in the church, it is critically important that we provide the appropriate training for those who have been outside the church and convert to Christian faith. In short, programs of Christian education in our churches should be able to provide ongoing training in Christian belief and practice throughout a person's life and should also be able to accommodate a person who converts at any stage of her or his life.

Second, as noted, catechesis/training must provide for training in both beliefs and practices that are central to the faith. The method that we noted from the early church, utilizing one of the traditional creeds, would cover all the areas that the broader Christian tradition has identified as essential beliefs. Surely, training in basic Christian doctrine would include at least five major areas. One, it would cover the doctrine of the Trinity. In addition to summarizing the church's teaching, it would cover the implications and importance of the trinitarian doctrine for our daily lives. For example, we would discuss the implications of our having been created in the image of God, who is deeply relational, consisting of three persons in perfectly loving relationships. Two, it would explore the two natures of Jesus. In teaching about the two natures, we would maintain balance, not over-emphasizing the human nature (putting at risk human salvation) or the divine nature (risking too great a separation from those of us who are called to imitate him in our daily living). Three, our catechesis would provide teaching on human nature. It would recognize that we are creatures, loved deeply by God, but also fallen and sinful. At the same time, our catechesis would explore God's intentions for us, both in this life and the next. Four, we would cover the concept of atonement—God's intervention in human history to reconcile all of creation to himself. While covering the different ways in which the church has described what happens in atonement, we would be sure to point out the contribution each makes to a rich understanding of the work and sacrifice of Christ. Finally, we would explore the doctrine of the church. As we noted earlier, the hope of the world is Jesus, and Jesus has established the church to bear his message to the world. What does it mean to say that Christ established the church as the primary mediator of God's presence in the world? What allegiance do we owe to the church and how do we empower it to require accountability of us? While we could easily identify other doctrines for which training would be good and important, these five constitute, in my view, a minimum doctrinal catechesis for empowering church members to live out faithfully the commitments made at their baptism.

Third, catechesis would need also to provide training in practices. This would include training on at least the common sacraments shared by virtually all followers of Jesus—baptism and Holy Communion. Beyond these sacraments, it would cover practices important to sustaining us in the life of faith. Inclusion of what John Wesley called "works of mercy" and "works of piety" would be one way to frame it. In addition to participation in Holy Communion, there are five other practices that Wesley identified as works of piety. They are prayer, searching the Scriptures (or, regular Bible study), fasting, Christian community (making sure we are regularly engaged with other Christians), and healthy living (along the lines of the scriptural injunction to offer ourselves as living sacrifices). Touching on the importance of each would be part of the overall catechetical training. Works of mercy are outwardly focused, aimed at engaging those around us. They include the general admonition to do good, visiting those sick and in prison, tending to the physical needs of the poor (feeding and clothing them, for example), hard work and philanthropy (characterized by Wesley as "earning all we can, saving all we can, so we can give away all that we can"), and opposition to all forms of slavery (given Wesley's day, this was particularly important; in our day, we might word this as opposition to all forms of exploitation and injustice).

If we intend to be, for example, good golfers, we expect to invest significant time and energy in perfecting the different aspects of the game. We will have to learn both theory and practice, and then we will have to engage in actually playing the game frequently, both to develop skills and to keep them sharp once developed. Should we expect any less if we wish to, as Wesley would say, "become perfect" in our love of God and neighbor?

The topic of catechesis deserves a book-length treatment all on its own. Here, I have only attempted to sketch an outline of what such a program would potentially look like. Granted, I have modeled what I propose both on the readings we examined from the early church as well as on my own Wesleyan context. For those in other traditions, I am sure that there exists a body of material for that tradition, which covers both essential Christian beliefs as well as important practices in which Christians are expected to engage. Take the time to do some research and locate those materials. If you have a role in the local church in educational programming, I urge you to become an advocate for deep and serious church training, aimed at educating and empowering Christians to live successfully the life of discipleship!

Part Two: Social Life

IV.

The Early Fathers on Human Freedom

I remember the discussion like it was yesterday. I was in my early seminary training. One of my professors and I had become good friends, and since we were neighbors, we often hung out in the evenings and discussed philosophy and theology. In the summers, we "philosophized" while shooting baskets; in the winter, we debated over friendly games of nine-ball. As Wesleyans, we were (and are!) firmly committed to the reality of human free will. Yet, in one evening's dialog, we were reflecting on writings by Luther (*The Bondage of the Will*), Augustine (particularly where he denied his own ability to freely choose to escape from his sins), and Calvin (perhaps the tradition's strongest advocate of the doctrine of predestination). I am not sure who said it first, but we both agreed that it was at least worth reflection that three of Christianity's great leaders had all expressed doubts about how free we humans really are. Essentially, Augustine and Luther argue that sin has so corrupted our free will that we are in bondage to it and can do nothing but sin prior to God's gracious intervention. Calvin, in turn, attempts to build these denials of free will into a set of doctrinal affirmations, all tied together into an overarching view of God, humans, and the world. As I indicated, we are both still firm believers in human freedom, even though the challenges these thinkers raise at least caught our attention.

As it turns out, John Wesley provides a way to hold together concerns raised by Luther and Augustine without accepting the Calvinist conclusion. Wesley observed that, at one point, he came within a hair's breadth of Calvin. What he meant was that he agreed that humans were naturally sinful and in bondage to sin. However, believing Arminius to be right about human freedom, he also affirmed that humans actually do have free will. How did he hold the two positions together? The key point is that Wesley claims that "natural humans" are in bondage to sin. However, he distinguishes between "natural humans" (which turns out to be the state of humanity after the Fall) and "actual humans" (which describes all humans as they are actually born into the world). Actual humans (the only kind that really exist) are immediately the recipients of God's prevenient grace. One of the main things that God's prevenient grace does is free us from our bondage to sin so that we can respond to God's call to us. In this way, Wesley argued that all living humans have free will, but the fact that they have free will is, itself, already a gift from God secured through Jesus. Neither my professor nor I found arguments for theological determinism (another phrase for the doctrine of predestination) or scientific determinism (the belief that all our choices are really the outcome of physical-chemical processing) convincing. However, one does not have to surrender the belief in free will altogether to express caution about the extent to which we are free. In other words, to say humans are free is not to say that human freedom has no boundaries.

A few years later under a different professor, I had a second conversation that deeply influenced my understanding of the ways in which Christians should understand human freedom. I had the good fortune to spend a term at the University of Munich studying under systematic theologian Wolfhart Pannenberg. My focus was on his doctrine of God.[1] In review of his writings, some critics argued that Pannenberg's theology left little room for human freedom. While I disagreed with that view, I felt the need to question him about it. As I became more pointed in my questioning, I recall a moment where he sat up straight in his chair and pointed a finger in my direction. He said, "Mr. Gutenson, we as Christians should not be primarily concerned with the notion of freedom as the ability to choose between options. No, we as Christians should be first concerned with a much more biblical notion of freedom, freedom in the sense of freedom from sin!"[2] He went on to talk about how Augustine had written of the paradox of freedom. The paradox, he said, was that as persons become more conformed to the image of Christ, they actually find the range of choices they might actually make becoming smaller. Freedom for Christians, he said, increasingly meant liberty from choosing sinful behaviors. In the midst of a world that has made "personal freedom" the ultimate good, Pannenberg sent me back to the early church for a better grasp of what it meant to be free.

During the early church period, particularly prior to Augustine, there was little question as to whether humans *possessed* free will. In fact, some explicitly argued that the entire concept of morality and moral accountability would make no sense apart from human freedom. Consider[3] Clement of Rome:

> For no other reason does God punish the sinner either in the present or future world, except because He knows that the sinner was able to conquer but neglected to gain the victory.[4]

Or, Justin Martyr:

> We have learned from the prophets, and we hold it to be true, that punishments, chastisements, and rewards are rendered according to the merit of each man's actions. Otherwise, if all things happen by fate, then nothing is in our own power. For if it be predestined that one man be good and another man evil, then the first is not deserving of praise or the other to be blamed. Unless humans have the power of avoiding evil and choosing good by free choice, they are not accountable for their actions—whatever they may be. . . .[5]

Or, Irenaeus:

> And in man, as well as in angels, [God] has placed the power of choice . . . so that those who had yielded obedience might justly possess what is good, given indeed by God, but preserved by themselves.[6]

However, for our purposes, we need not pursue whether humans possess free will. As a Wesleyan, I will consider its plausibility adequately demonstrated by numerous writings. The freedom of the will itself is not so much the question for us as is the question implied by the statement from Pannenberg above. Specifically, the question is: of the different ways in which one can understand the term *freedom*, which has highest priority for us as Christians? And, true to our method, how does the early church guide us? While Augustine *may* go further than I do in denying free will, he still has numerous things to say that help us prioritize the different senses of freedom.

Augustine was born in 354 and died a few months short of his seventy-sixth birthday in 430. The early church fathers are often divided into Eastern and Western fathers, and many agree in judging Augustine the greatest of the Western fathers. To see the extent of his contribution to the Christian faith, one only need note that of the popular thirty-eight-volume collection of the writings of the early church, eight contain some of his works. Augustine was born in what is now Algeria to a pagan father and a Christian mother. Her name was Monica and she, too, would later be considered by the church to be a saint. While Monica attempted to raise her son as a Christian, he deeply disappointed her when he became a follower of the dualistic sect Manicheism. During the early period of his life, as we know from his famous autobiography *The Confessions*, Augustine pursued a life of pleasure. His tongue-in-cheek prayer from this period is well known: "Grant me chastity and continence, but not yet."[7] As we will see, in *The Confessions*, Augustine often observed his inability to overcome his sinful nature, always losing out to his baser self.

When he was thirty, the imperial court in Milan employed Augustine as a professor of rhetoric, one of the most prized academic positions in the world. His mother moved with him to Milan and he came under the influence of the local bishop, Ambrose. Between the influence of Ambrose, his mother, and his studies in Neoplatonism, Augustine became increasingly open to the Christian faith. As a result, in the summer of 386, he underwent a deep and profound conversion that led him to give up his career in rhetoric, including surrendering his prized teaching position, and to commit himself to the service of God. Notwithstanding his earlier hedonism, he turned to the priesthood and readily embraced the vow of celibacy. The story of his conversion is one of the best known of Christian history. It is worth letting him tell it in his own words:

> I cast myself down I know not how, under a certain fig-tree, giving full vent to my tears; and the floods of mine eyes gushed out an acceptable sacrifice to Thee. And, not indeed in these words, yet to this purpose, spake I much unto Thee: and Thou, O Lord, how long? how long, Lord, wilt Thou be angry for ever? Remember not our former iniquities, for I felt that I was held by them. I sent up these sorrowful words: How long, how long, "tomorrow, and tomorrow?" Why not now? why not is there this hour an end to my uncleanness? So was I speaking and weeping in the most bitter contrition of my heart, when, lo! I heard from a neighbouring house a voice, as of boy or girl, I know not, chanting, and oft repeating, "Take up and read; Take up and read." Instantly, my countenance altered, I began to think most intently whether children were wont in any kind of play to sing such words: nor could I remember ever to have heard the like. So checking the torrent of my tears, I arose; interpreting it to be no other than a command from God to open the book, and read the first chapter I should find. For I had heard of Antony, that coming in during the reading of the Gospel, he received the admonition, as if what was being read was spoken to him: Go, sell all that thou hast, and give to the poor, and thou shalt have treasure in heaven, and come and follow me: and by such oracle he was forthwith converted unto Thee. Eagerly then I returned to the place where Alypius was sitting; for there had I laid the volume of the Apostle when I arose thence. I seized, opened, and in silence read that section

> on which my eyes first fell: Not in rioting and drunkenness, not in chambering and wantonness, not in strife and envying; but put ye on the Lord Jesus Christ, and make not provision for the flesh, in concupiscence. No further would I read; nor needed I: for instantly at the end of this sentence, by a light as it were of serenity infused into my heart, all the darkness of doubt vanished away.[8]

One only need skim the record of his life and his writings to sense the depth of conversion of life Augustine experienced. Throughout, he maintained that his ability to overcome sin and respond to God's call was a gift of pure grace and not a thing he could have done on his own. Let us see what Augustine can do to help us understand rightly human freedom, a concept, sadly, often poorly articulated from a Christian and biblical perspective.

In our contemporary context, it is hard to imagine a word more frequently tossed around to arouse our passions than the word *freedom.* I have to admit that my suspicions are raised immediately when I see some new congressional legislation with the word *freedom* in it or when I hear a public official affirm that some action is being undertaken to honor or expand our freedoms. Too often, the term is co-opted and deployed in a very Orwellian way so that if one takes the time to dig into the legislation or claims being made, one frequently finds the meaning to be the opposite of the normal sense. Whenever someone aims to promote a particular agenda, he or she often tries to find a way to frame the agenda as a "freedom" issue by appealing to our fundamental American value of freedom in the sense of liberty to choose.

And, why not? Does not our existence as a people itself rest in the very appeal to the notion of freedoms and liberties? The founding documents of the United States of America speak of certain "unalienable rights" and go on to say these include "liberty and the pursuit of happiness." The desire for freedom, or the right to be the "captain of our own souls," extends beyond the American tradition and runs deep in the human soul. It does so particularly in the contemporary West. I affirm that the right to exercise our freedom of choice is an important and good thing, yet I also have to ask whether this particular sense of freedom has the highest priority within the biblical narrative. Is it really the case, in other words, that God's biggest concern, when it comes to human freedom, is to make sure that we all are free to do as we please? I think the answer to that question is no. In fact, the Western notion of freedom, while in general a good thing, is more a product of Enlightenment individualism on the one hand and the political philosophy of John Locke on the other. Biblically speaking, anytime the Scriptures use the phrase "each person did what they thought to be right," it is uniformly a bad thing.

Individual Liberty: Freedom to Choose

It is critically important to note that there are at least three ways in which freedom has been understood. First, there is freedom to choose any one of a range of options open to us. I will call this sense the freedom to choose. Where do I choose to live? What will I do with my life and its resources? Will I pursue my own interest or the common good? Will I drive a big car or a small one? Live in a large house or a modest one? This is the common meaning of the word *freedom* we deploy in everyday American life. At the core of our democracy is the idea that self-determination is one of the greatest goods—the idea that our lives are our own and we should be free to do with them as we choose. As suggested above, it is embodied in freedom for "the pursuit of happiness." And, of course, this sense of freedom *is* important. It moves from being a good thing to being problematic when separated from the other two senses or when it is elevated above them. If we improperly relate these senses of freedom, we risk inverting the moral obligations that the different senses of freedom rightly impose on us.

Ontological Freedom: Freedom to Be

The second sense of freedom is one that I take from the older philosophical tradition, dating back at least to Aristotle. According to Aristotle, a thing is free to the extent it is able to align with its *telos*—its end, its purpose. I will call this ontological sense of freedom the freedom to be. Every person, by reason of his or her unique nature, has been created with a particular end or goal, according to Aristotle. So, in this tradition, a thing, or a person, is free not as a consequence of his or her self-determination or because he or she has more or fewer choices available. Rather, freedom comes as a consequence of having removed the obstacles that prevent a person from aligning with his or her reason for being. Paradoxically, more often freedom in this sense means fewer choices. We become freer as we find fewer choices actually open to us, because choice becomes disciplined by our *telos* or end.

Implicitly recognized, at least among Christians, is the likelihood that we humans will choose badly. By choosing badly, we place ourselves on paths that lead us away from our purpose. We do not become freer even if we have more choices available to us! Instead, we find that we become more a slave to the obstacles that prevent us from reaching our purpose, obstacles of our own choosing, derived, no doubt, from our own desires and hungers. There is an illusion of "freedom," but it is just that.

Spiritual Freedom: Freedom from Sin

The third sense of freedom is closely related to the freedom to be. In fact, perhaps it is an explicitly Christian version of the freedom to be. As Pannenberg said, we Christians ought first to be concerned about a spiritual "freedom from sin." He observed to me that we have, for example in St. Augustine, the paradoxical notion that as a person becomes freer in this sense, he or she finds that one's "life choices" decrease rather than increase. That is, as we become more Christlike, as we increasingly embody God's love, we find the range of choices open to us narrowing. Instead, we become empowered more and more to choose the right in each situation. We paradoxically become freer even while our range of real choices declines, because the freedom from sin and the freedom to choose often initially run in opposite directions. Consider the example of petty theft, which is a real option for some. As our discipleship deepens and we are increasingly conformed to the image of Christ, we find that sinful behaviors, such as theft, cease to be real options for us. The licentious period of Augustine's life granted him many choices, pleasures, and opportunities to act in what he took to be his own self-interest. However, the choices he made bound him seemingly more and more tightly to his lust. When he was freed from those sins, many of the old choices did not exist anymore. Yet, he was freer to be all God had intended him to be.

If this still sounds strange, consider this question: will we be free in heaven, when God's kingdom is fully realized? Surely the answer is yes, emphatically so. But we Christians agree that the former life will have passed and with it, the possibility of embracing our past sins. The kind of freedom we will enjoy in heaven is not the freedom of choices, but rather the freedom from the sins that beset us.

If we think about this carefully, it becomes obvious that the form of freedom most popular in the West, that is, the freedom to choose, can never by itself be adequate as a Christian account of freedom. According to the Scriptures, God's goal for us is reconciliation and conversion, a conversion that makes us new people. What characterizes this newness is a freedom from our sins in order to live as God intends. Each of the three kinds of freedom is important and good, but they must be held in right relation if we are to properly and holistically speak of freedom. As suggested, my concern is that American civil discourse has deified the first sense of freedom, the freedom to choose, and has largely forgotten the importance of the other two. I agree with Pannenberg—we Christians need to focus much more on becoming free from sin and spend much less time and attention making sure we are all free to "do what is right in our own sight."

It is worth noting that we are seeing a resurgence in the West, and particularly in America, of a political ideology called "libertarianism." While there are different strands with different emphases, the basic idea of libertarianism is that liberty to do as we please is the highest good. Libertarians believe that political and social structures should be set up so as to maximize liberty and to minimize obligations that we have toward one another. Laws, for the most part, should exist to protect our "stuff," but libertarians generally hold that laws should not exist to create a social safety net for those on the margins. I must admit that I find it puzzling how Christians are able to embrace such a political ideology. The Scriptures teach us that we have obligations (serious obligations, if one reads Matthew 25, for example) to those who are poor and on the margins. Yet, libertarianism would suggest that those obligations are purely voluntary, to be undertaken if we feel so inclined. What such a position essentially claims is that to God, it is more important that I be free to do with my resources whatever I please than that there be laws that require some basic level of care and support for the poor. We will return to these themes when we get to the chapter on wealth and poverty in the early church. But, for here, I can only echo my earlier comment that it is hard for me to see how Christians can believe that libertarianism, in its commonly understood form, is consistent with the teachings of the Scriptures and the early church.

As we noted earlier, Augustine realized the critical nature of the freedom from sin and spoke of it frequently, particularly in regard to John 8:36. Here, Jesus is talking to some of those who are attacking his ministry. At verse 36, he says, "Therefore, if the Son makes you free, you really will be free." But, which sense of freedom does he mean? Is he speaking of the liberty to choose? Consider Augustine's words from his homilies on St. John, just after citing verse 36:

> Our hope is this, brethren, to be made free by the free One; and that, in setting us free, He may make us His servants. For we were the servants of lust, but being set free, we are made the servants of love. This also, the apostle says, "for, brethren, ye have been called into liberty, only use not liberty for an occasion to the flesh, but by love

> serve [one] another." Let not then the Christian say, I am free; I have been redeemed, and by my very redemption have been made free, I shall do what I please; no one may balk me of my will, if I am free. But if thou committest with such a will, thou art the servant of sin. . . .
>
> The first stage of liberty, then, is to be free from crimes [sinful conduct]. When a man has begun to be free from these (and every Christian man ought to be so), he begins to raise his head to liberty; but that is liberty begun, not completed. Why, says some one, is it not completed liberty? Because, "I see another law in my members warring against the law of my mind"; "for what I would," he says, "that do I not; but what I hate, that do I." . . . In part liberty, in part bondage; not yet entire, not yet pure, not yet full liberty, because not yet eternity.[9]

Later, in the *Enchiridion*, he takes up the theme again:

> . . . what kind of liberty, I ask, can the bond-slave possess, except when it pleases him to sin? For [he] is freely in bondage who does with pleasure the will of his master. Accordingly, he who is the servant of sin is free to sin. And hence he will not be free to do right, until, being freed from sin, he shall begin to be the servant of righteousness. And this is true liberty, for he has pleasure in the righteous deed, *and it is at the same time a holy bondage* [emphasis added], for he is obedient to the will of God. But whence comes this liberty to do right to the man who is in bondage and sold under sin, except he be redeemed by Him who has said, "If the Son shall make you free, ye shall be free indeed."[10]

Augustine clearly, from a Christian perspective, sees an order and a priority for the differing kinds of freedom. The reason Augustine has low regard for the sense of freedom we called the "freedom to choose" was because his strong doctrine of an inherently sinful human nature led him to conclude that "freedom to choose" would inevitably lead to choosing badly. He had experienced it in his own life, he read it in the Scriptures, and he saw it in others. It was a normative idea for him. To the extent humans were "free to choose," they were free to choose badly. In fact, Augustine explicitly ties human freedom to the Fall when he says, "it was by the evil use of his free-will that man destroyed both it and himself."[11]

According to Augustine, the more we use our free will or our liberty to engage in sinful behaviors, the more we are enslaved to those sinful behaviors. The freer we become in our ability to choose, the more we are enslaved to sin; the more we are enslaved to Christ, with its inherent restriction on evil choices, the freer we really become. Augustine explicitly recognized what we as twenty-first-century folk seem thoroughly unable to grasp: the fact that left to ourselves, to do as we think right, our own selfishness and desires will inevitably result in our making bad or sinful choices. We are seduced to accept the concept of the liberty to choose as the greatest good and, thereby, turn a blind eye to our own sinful natures.

We can clarify and expand this a little by way of St. Thomas Aquinas. He described a habit as a settled tendency to use a faculty in a particular way, either for good or for evil. We are a sinful people embedded in and among a sinful people and we too often use our faculties in pursuit of our own self-interests. As we continue and develop that tendency, it becomes established in us as a habit. Aquinas, then, gives us a glimpse into the process whereby we become enslaved. Bad choices in how we use our faculties reinforce similar use in the future. We repeat the trend until it becomes a settled disposition and, thus, we have become enslaved to sin. Choose as we will, Aquinas would say, and we will overwhelmingly choose badly.

Consider the connections between the second and third senses of freedom; that is, the freedom to be and the freedom from sin. Why is it that God desires to free us from our sin? Is it merely an abstract notion of being sinless that motivates God's focus here? God has created us with certain ends in mind for us. I have written elsewhere on this in more detail.[12] God has created us first and foremost for loving relationship with God and for living in loving relationships with those around us. In fact, the end goal God has in mind for us is relationships of mutual interdependence, where we judge the interests of others as more important than our own. Within this, we are called to give particular attention to those whom the Scriptures reference as "the least of these" or those otherwise on the margins and vulnerable. To realize this as our end, our God-intended telos, is to realize that to pursue the *freedom to be* cannot be an individual goal, but must include seeking first and foremost to remove all obstacles that would stand in the way of that telos for others, even before ourselves.

Obviously, then, one cannot be an advocate of the *freedom to be* or the freedom from sin without becoming engaged in the struggle for liberation and justice for all those for whom systems and other factors hamper their ability to become all God made them to be. Once again, the freedom to be serves as a buttress and corrective to the freedom to choose, and the freedom to choose and the freedom of self-determination are rightly disciplined by the recognition of the end goal of God's creative activity.

For Christians, Augustine gives us a clear summary of what constitutes freedom:

> And as it is certainly true, what kind of liberty, I ask, can the bond-slave possess, except when it pleases him to sin? For [he] is freely in bondage who does with pleasure the will of his master. Accordingly, he who is the servant of sin is free to sin. And hence he will not be free to do right, until, being freed from sin, he shall begin to be the servant of righteousness. *And this is true liberty, for he has pleasure in the righteous deed, and it is at the same time a holy bondage, for he is obedient to the will of God.* [emphasis added]

Augustine gives us the test of genuine freedom: that we love to do what is right. He again makes explicit the paradox—lots of liberty to do as we please leads to enslavement to sin, but being freed by the Son from our sinful habits and from our baser self offers genuine freedom, even as it restricts our options. But, notice that Augustine calls this Christian sense of freedom *holy bondage.* Consider the words of the song by Bob Dylan from many years back:

> Well, it may be the devil or it may be the Lord
> But you're gonna have to serve somebody.[13]

Holy bondage? Demonic bondage? Perhaps these are the only real choices when it comes to the subject of human freedom.

Ideas to Consider

As we conclude this discussion, five points are worth summary attention.

1. I have affirmed the reality of human freedom and argued that humans are not predestined to do what they do.

2. I have denied that the ability to choose freely is inherently a bad thing. In fact, I have argued it is a good thing.
3. I have reminded us that, as believers in the doctrine of original sin, we must recognize that our freedom in the sense of liberty to choose must be disciplined and, thus, give way to higher priorities—namely, escaping from sin.
4. I have argued, along with Augustine, Aquinas, and others that, from a Christian perspective, the highest of all freedoms is the freedom to be delivered from our sins. Without that, our freedom to choose will inevitably fail us and draw us into bondage to sin. This means that we, twenty-first-century Christians, must exercise a good deal of caution, lest we join the spirit of the age in elevating personal liberty to a priority not supported by the Scriptures or the early church.
5. We must recognize the far-reaching implications of making freedom from sin our highest goal. To be free from sin is to be free from the need to make our own interests sacrosanct. It frees us to obey Christ's command to elevate the interest of others over our own. In a world where this is true, there can be no slavery, no exploitation, and no profiting at the expense of others. These exploitative and manipulative behaviors, justified when "freedom to choose" is the highest good, must be disciplined by obedience to love. Not an abstract love, but the flesh-and-blood kind Jesus spoke of when he said, of the blessed, "I was hungry and you gave me food to eat. I was thirsty and you gave me a drink. . . . I was naked and you gave me clothes to wear" (Matthew 25:35-36). May it be the case that the Son makes us free so that we might be free indeed!

V.

The Early Fathers on Wealth and Poverty

Maybe you have heard words such as these:

"Look out for number one."

"What's mine is mine, and what's yours is yours."

"If I elevated the interests of others over my own, I'd soon be in poverty myself."

"Talk of economic justice is just disguised talk of socialism and communism."

These statements express common sentiments among many sections of our society. We seem largely to be believers in the "rugged individualism" of a past age—a rugged individualism that is often credited with giving birth to our country and its prevailing set of values and commitments. The question with which Christians must occupy themselves, though, is whether these common sentiments are consistent with being faithful followers of Jesus. Does the gospel call us to a rugged individualism that largely separates our own well-being from that of our neighbor—an individualism that seems to relieve us of challenging obligations that seem so apparent in the Scriptures? Is it really the case that as Christians we can be motivated by the sentiment "what is mine is mine . . ."?

As with so many questions about what the gospel means and how these meanings are to be lived out in our daily lives, the answer you get varies depending on whom you ask. The answer a person gives to any of these questions likely boils down to how he or she reads the Scriptures and judges the merits of the arguments used to defend or critique such sentiments. So, the question becomes: who understands the Scriptures rightly? Or, if the Scriptures are not the primary source for making a determination on sentiments such as these, then what or who is? And, if the Scriptures are not the ultimate authority on these matters, then why is it that something else is?

We could take any of numerous tacks to answer these questions, but our goal is a simpler one. As with our stated intent, we want to pause and allow voices from the early church to speak to us. We want to allow those closer to the New Testament world to weigh in on issues of wealth and poverty. We want to allow them to influence the nuances we consider as we come to conclusions about this important part of the life of faith. Don't be surprised if what you hear sounds foreign and challenges much of what might be considered the prevailing wisdom today. It was, after all, a very different time with different values and priorities in play—different values and priorities that, in many cases, turn those of our own time on their head. Let us begin with that early church father known as Basil the Great.

Basil the Great was born into a wealthy family in the early part of the fourth century. His father was also named Basil and, in order to distinguish father and son, the father was known as Basil the Elder. If ever there were a person who enjoyed a "Christian pedigree," surely it was Basil the Great. His grandmother is known in church history as Macrina the Elder, and she and her husband suffered under the persecution of Christians at the hands of Maximinus Galerius prior to the time of Constantine. Her husband, Basil the Great's grandfather, ultimately became a martyr. Basil the Elder and his wife, Emmelia, had ten children. Incredibly, five are known to us as saints of the church. While Basil the Elder never served in the episcopacy, his family has had a remarkable influence on church history. Basil the Great and his brother, Gregory of Nyssa, along with Basil's friend, Gregory of Nazianzus, comprised that group of early theologians known as the Cappadocian fathers. They were profoundly instrumental in working out the church's statement of the trinitarian doctrine formalized in the Creed of Constantinople in 381. The other three siblings of Basil and Gregory that have attained the status of saint are Peter of Sabaste, Naucratius, and Macrina the Younger. Basil's education was carried out by his father and grandmother, Macrina, who had herself studied at the feet of another of the early church fathers, Gregory Thaumaturgus (sometimes known as Gregory the Wonderworker).

In his early twenties, Basil underwent a conversion of life. While trained for and initially beginning a practice in law and rhetoric, Basil abandoned that career for a life of devotion to God. He later wrote:

> I had wasted much time on follies and spent nearly all of my youth in vain labors, and devotion to the teachings of a wisdom that God had made foolish. Suddenly, I awoke as out of a deep sleep. I beheld the wonderful light of the Gospel truth, and I recognized the nothingness of the wisdom of the princes of this world.[1]

Consistent with this new life of discipleship, Basil distributed his wealth to the poor and soon launched a monastic settlement on his family estate where members of his family and other like-minded folks joined him. Later, Basil became Bishop of Caesarea and used his inheritance to serve the poor of his parish. Near Caesarea, he built a large complex that served as a hospital, a hospice care center, and a poorhouse. He died before turning fifty, but this complex remained a monument to the seriousness with which he took his obligations to those less fortunate than he. Let's take a look at some of the things he had to say about wealth and poverty.

Perhaps you are familiar with the parable of the barns (sometimes called the parable of the rich fool) from Luke 12. The story is straightforward. A rich man had a particularly good year and enjoyed a harvest so great that he did not have adequate storage facilities. Here was a remarkably successful entrepreneur who had wisely leveraged his resources for maximum return. To take full advantage of his combination of good fortune and wise business management, he did what any of us might do. He planned to build bigger storage facilities for his goods and to take an early retirement. That's what we are supposed to do, right? Use our skills to maximize profits in order to lay up for ourselves a future of ease. Or as the rich man said to himself: "Take it easy! Eat, drink, and enjoy yourself" (Luke 12:19). This businessman had succeeded in realizing the twenty-first-century dream: develop a highly profitable business and use that to take care of number one. This is a common way for us to see things, and it is hard for us to fully appreciate the judgment Jesus announces. The man is not a wise man at all. In fact, Jesus says that God judges him to be a fool. Why? Because he had failed to see that his success was not to be taken as an opportunity to take life easy, but rather that his success was to be used to benefit others. While it is hard for us to hear the parable read this way, it was not hard at all for Basil. Consider this from his commentary on the parable:

> Unhappy ones that you are! What answer will you make to the Great Judge? You cover with tapestry the bareness of your walls, and do not clothe the nakedness of men. You adorn your steeds with most rich and costly trappings, and despise your brother who is in rags. You allow the corn in your granaries to rot or be eaten up by vermin, and you deign not even to cast a glance on those who have no bread. You hoard your wealth, and do not deign to look upon those who are worn and oppressed by necessity! You will say to me: "What wrong do I commit if I hoard that which is mine?" And I ask you: "Which are the things that you think belong to you? From whom did you receive them? You act like a man who being in a theatre, and having seized upon the places that others might have taken, seeks to prevent every one else from entering, applying to his own use that which should be for the use of all." And thus it is with the rich, who having been the first to obtain possession of those things which should be common to all, appropriate them to themselves and retain them in their possession; for if each one took only what is necessary for his subsistence, and gave the rest to the indigent, there would be neither rich nor poor.[2]

Or, consider this somewhat different translation, beginning and ending in slightly different places:

> "Whom do I injure," [the rich person] says, "when I retain and conserve my own?" Which things, tell me, are yours? Whence have you brought them into being? You are like one occupying a place in a theatre, who should prohibit others from entering, treating that as one's own which was designed for the common use of all.
>
> Such are the rich. Because they were first to occupy common goods, they take these goods as their own. If each one would take that which is sufficient for one's needs, leaving what is in excess to those in distress, no one would be rich, no one poor.
>
> Did you not come naked from the womb? Will you not return naked into the earth? (Job 1:21). Whence then did you have your present possessions? If you say, "By chance," you are godless, because you do not acknowledge the Creator, nor give thanks to the Giver. If you admit they are from God, tell us why you have received them.
>
> Is God unjust to distribute the necessaries of life to us unequally? Why are you rich, why is that one poor? Is it not that you may receive the reward of beneficence and faithful distribution . . .?[3]

Basil's take on the significance of the parable is a bit more, shall we say, concrete than our often overly abstract readings—readings that too often reduce these words of Jesus to being more about "attitudes of the heart" than about actual behaviors.

Notice how Basil characterizes the rich man's success. First, he quickly dismisses the idea that the rich man's successes are his own. When the rich man observes that he merely wishes to enjoy what is the product of his own labors, Basil asks him what, exactly, is his.

The rich man did not bring his crops into being (he used the good and fertile earth that God has provided for all). Therefore, he cannot claim them as his own. It is unlikely that Basil would have denied that, in John Locke's words, the man had mixed his own labor with these raw materials. But for Basil that was hardly enough to justify the man's claim to a right to hoard his produce. Undoubtedly, had the man responded in this way, Basil would have observed that even the man's ability to work, his intellect and good health, were not "his" in any absolute sense. Rather, these, too, came to the farmer as gifts from God. The Apostle Paul would have been sympathetic to this way of reading things, asking as he does in 1 Corinthians 4: "What is it that you have that does not have the status of a gift from God?" (paraphrased). One has to marvel at how easily these early Christians understood every aspect of their lives as a gift from God and, as such, carried much deeper obligations than we contemporaries realize. With such a way of evaluating things, the stern warnings of the pericope of the Great Judgment in the second half of Matthew 25 become much clearer, do they not?

Later, at the end of this section, Basil drives the point home. First, he cites the words from Job that remind us that we came into the world with nothing and we will surely leave it with nothing. Did we come by our successes by chance? If we say that, we are pagans for not acknowledging God's gracious gifts to us. If we say they are from God, then Basil asks why we have received them. Why is it the farmer, in particular, has been the beneficiary of this success? His answer? God is not unjust for distributing life's necessities to folks in different proportion. On the contrary, blessings have come our way in order that we might receive the blessing that comes from distributing our wealth to those less fortunate. In making these points, of course, Basil expresses a significant strand of biblical teaching that says that God blesses, not so that we might hoard blessings, but rather so that we might be a blessing to others. As early as Genesis, God reminds us that the gift of blessing is never merely for our own good. Instead, it is so that we might turn it into blessing for others less fortunate. While he does not make the connection here, one could also cite the biblical claim that from those to whom much is given, much is required. It is an explicit connection of God's blessing (in this case, of the farmer's work) to God's expectation (to be a blessing) then finally to God's judgment (here, the very life of the farmer who misunderstood the reason for his successes). It sounds very odd to our ears, doesn't it—this idea that, in God's sight, what we earn by our own labors is not just ours to do with as we please? Let's consider some other "strange" words from Basil on the subject of wealth and poverty.

Later in the same sermon, Basil writes:

> Who is the greedy person? It's him, who doesn't content himself with what he has. And who [is] the thief? He who steals what belongs to others. And you think that you are not greedy, and that you do not rob others? What had been granted to you so that you might care for others, you claim for yourself.
>
> He who strips a man of his clothes is to be called a thief. Is not he who, when he is able, fails to clothe the naked, worthy of no other title? The bread which you do not use is the bread of the hungry; the garment hanging in your wardrobe is the garment of him who is naked; the shoes that you do not wear are the shoes of the one who is barefoot; the money that you keep locked away is the money

of the poor; the acts of charity that you do not perform are so many injustices that you commit.[4]

Let us examine how Basil characterizes the unwillingness to use one's resources for the good of the less fortunate, and in particular notice how out of step his idea is with our twenty-first-century way of thinking about these issues.

Basil starts with the concept of greed and asks us to consider, along with him, what constitutes greed. He moves from there directly to the concept of theft. Then, he makes the direct connection. Who is greedy? The one who is not content with enough. Who is the thief? The one who takes what is rightly another's. Then, we get to the consequence that he draws—we are greedy and we are robbers when we do not use what we have been able to gain for the benefit of others. Basil thinks that, in God's sight, it is just as much theft when someone fails to use his or her resources to benefit those in need as it is when someone breaks in and takes what belongs to another.

This point is worth pondering for a moment. We have no problem with Basil's affirmation that the one who takes another person's clothes is a thief, but he does not stop there. Basil says I can also be a thief merely by refusing to use the extra clothing I have to clothe the one in need. By hoarding the excess for myself, I rob from the one who has too little. Then, in the second paragraph, he expands and gets more explicit—if you have leftover bread, then it belongs to the hungry; unused clothing or shoes are rightly the property of those who need them. One has to wonder, then, if we followed Basil's words here, would we not see the property rights of the poor very differently, but just as seriously as we do when we protect the property rights of the rich? He summarizes: when we do not do the acts of charity that we could, these are injustices that we commit. Then, to put this back in the context of the passage from Luke, the injustices we commit draw God's ire and, ultimately, God's judgment. How hard is that for us steeped in the values and priorities of the twenty-first century to hear?

It is worth thinking about why Basil characterizes things in this way. Is it, for example, because in the economic systems of his time, one's acquisition of wealth and property came at the cost of someone else? In other words, is Basil making a judgment concerning how wealth was acquired in his day, on the backs of the poor and less fortunate? It matters, some would say, because we live in a very different economic environment, one in which it is not always the case that wealth is brokered through exploitation of others. However, as you look at his words closely, this is really not the sense you come away with—there is no evidence that exploitation of workers was an issue here at all. It seems Basil is making no judgment about how the wealth was acquired; rather the entire matter is one of how wealth is utilized. If I have wealth, and I deploy it only for my own enjoyment, then I am robbing from those less fortunate—I am engaging in theft from the needy, who have, according to Basil, every right to expect that I utilize my luxuries to relieve their suffering. Basil does not see this beneficence as something optional that we do "if we feel like it"; instead, he couches this distribution of our goods as an obligation we have before God.

How do we deal with these claims? Dismiss them as from an age far too antiquated to matter to us today? Or, do we take time to reflect on the extent to which we may have missed the radical nature of Christ's call on our lives? It is very easy to provide reasons why these words need not be taken seriously today, but I encourage us to take time to really hear them and consider the possibility that these early fathers were on to something—something important about how God sees our wealth and possessions, something about how God expects us to order our lives and the utilization of those resources. What can we learn from Basil, Augustine, and others who thought this way?

Let us quickly hear a number of other representatives from the early church on this same issue. From St. John Chrysostom's *Homily on Romans*:

> If you wish to leave much wealth to your children, leave them in God's care. For he who without your having done anything, gave you a soul, and formed you a body, and granted you the gift of life, when he sees you displaying such munificence, and distributing your goods, must surely open to them all kinds of riches. . . . Do not leave them riches, but virtue and skill. For if they have the confidence of riches, they will not mind anything besides, for they shall have the means of screening the wickedness of their ways in their abundant riches.[5]

How many of us as parents take it for granted that accumulating riches to be left to our children is a good and salutary thing to do? Well, this particular fourth-century preacher seemed to think it not the wisest and most beneficent thing we could do for them. Notice part of John's rationale. If we leave wealth to our children, they will have the "confidence of riches," that is, they will not so easily be aware of their dependence on God. But notice what he goes on to say: by having wealth, they will be able to obscure from themselves their own wickedness. In other words, wealth will make it possible to get away with wickedness often without bearing the consequences, and in the end, not even realizing it as wickedness. And, just in case we think that those who preached this way in the early church were never attacked by the wealthy for their audacity, consider this observation from the very same John Chrysostom:

> I am criticized often for my continual attacks on the rich. Yes: because the rich continually attack the poor.[6]

It seems it was as much the case then as now that those who were well-to-do did not like it particularly well when they were reminded of the obligations that attended wealth. There seemed, however, to be no ambiguity in John's mind about where he should take his stand on these issues—on the side that recognized and defended the plight of the least fortunate.

A contemporary of Basil, specifically, his brother, the early saint now known as Gregory of Nyssa, once commented about the relative challenges of the New Testament as compared to the Old:

> Some think that the Old Testament is stricter than the New, but they judge wrongly; they are fooling themselves. The Old Law did not punish the desire to hold on to wealth; it punished theft. But now the rich man is not condemned for taking the property of others; rather, he is condemned for not giving his property away.[7]

Gregory amplifies Basil's sentiments as he observes that the New Testament intensifies the Old Testament's attitudes toward wealth when the New Testament condemns the wealthy for not freely giving what they have to the poor. How often have we heard words like these from our pulpits today? How often have you heard the words of Basil or

Augustine or Gregory on matters concerning our wealth and how we use it? We hear the obligations that attend wealth as stated in the New Testament spiritualized away so that they are more about "attitudes of the heart." Instead, they are about actual, concrete action. It is no surprise at all that we see and hear the Scriptures differently than our early forebears. Søren Kierkegaard, a Danish Christian philosopher, once said that the New Testament is really not so hard to understand on issues like this. The real issue, he went on to say, is that we just don't want to live the way the New Testament describes for us.

Consider St. John Chrysostom again, this time on laziness:

> "Anyone who would not work should not eat" (2 Thessalonians 3:10). . . . But the laws of Saint Paul are not merely for the poor. They are for the rich as well. . . . We accuse the poor of laziness. This laziness is often excusable. We ourselves are often guilty of worse idleness.[8]

John is right, is he not, that we often hear this passage recited with regard to the poor or the unemployed, yet we do not often hear it cited more broadly. John reminds us that laziness is not a sin just of the poor.

Moving on, Ambrose sounds a lot like Basil when he writes:

> You are not making a gift of your possessions to the poor person. You are handing over to him what is his.[9]

Ambrose also sees those things we hold as luxuries as belonging to those who are in need of them. Irenaeus takes it a step further when he reminds us that our beneficence is not merely to go to those with whom we share affinity. What is the paradigm case for love of the other according to the Scriptures?

> And instead of the tithes which the law commanded, the Lord said to divide everything we have with the poor. And he said to love not only our neighbors but also our enemies, and to be givers and sharers not only with the good but also to be liberal givers toward those who take away our possessions.[10]

To do what Irenaeus suggests here would be to set ourselves up to be taken advantage of, don't you think? Really, how could we be liberal givers to the very ones who would rob from us? Perhaps Irenaeus would cite Jesus: "Jesus looked at them carefully and said, 'It's impossible for human beings. But all things are possible for God'" (Matthew 19:26). And, evidently, Irenaeus took the words of Jesus to the rich young ruler to apply to all of his followers.

Hear, finally, the words of Pope Leo the Great, in commentary on the second half of Matthew 25, the pericope of the Great Judgment:

> When the Son of Man comes in majesty, when he sits on the throne of glory, when all people are gathered and he divides the good from the bad, what praise will he give those on his right hand? He will praise them only for works of kindness and charity; he will hold them as done for himself. For the One who made our nature his own did not hold himself back in any way from the most simple human thing. And what curse will there be for those on his left hand? Only that they neglected love; that they were inhumanly harsh and denied mercy to the oppressed. It is as though there were no other virtues with the first group, and as though there were no other sins than those of the other.[11]

Notice the theme of imitating Christ that Leo implies: our Lord, "the One who made our nature his own," gave himself freely for us in every way. Those who find favor in the Great Judgment, Leo writes, are those who have imitated Christ in this way, those who have found virtue in relieving the oppressed and easing the suffering of the poor. He concludes that what we see in the judgment of Matthew 25 is as if there were no other virtues than beneficence and liberality with regard to distribution of our goods and no other sins than greedy and selfish inaction in the face of suffering. Sobering thoughts, these.

So, what are we to do with all these "strange words"? That is the question, isn't it? We can be amazed or perhaps even amused at these words. I have had folks say to me outright, "Why, these passages cannot mean what they seem to—who could live that way?" It is hard not to marvel how, on the one hand, we hold the Scriptures with such piety and on the other hand, so easily dismiss them when they challenge us to do what we wish not to do. Yet, the question remains: what are we to do about these words from the early church? Ought we to go out tomorrow and sell all that we have and distribute it to the poor? My answer here is essentially the same as it is at the end of most every chapter. I cannot say how these words should impact you, the individual reader. I cannot say how God's call to give ourselves for the poor should be worked out in the lives of different followers of Jesus. What I can say, however, is this: we should ponder the words of our early sisters and brothers. We should let them sink in, and perhaps germinate, under the guidance of God's Holy Spirit. Perhaps under that good hand of guidance, we will again find what Jesus observed to be true—what is impossible for us is possible for God, and he may yet free us and empower us to live our lives "for the other" in ways we never even considered.

VI.

Stewardship of Creation

During the early church period, there were no major ecological crises to spur the church's attention to stewardship of God's creation. While famines, disease, and the like contributed from time to time to worries about the food supply,[1] the world's population was probably just over 200 million by the end of the sixth century.[2] Ecological concerns directly related to population were still a long way off.

Oil refinery processes had not yet been developed. There were no internal combustion engines around to generate the related pollutants. The potential environmental damage associated with mountaintop removal techniques used to mine coal and the long-distance transportation of crude oil had not yet been imagined. Debates about global warming and ozone depletion were centuries away, as were concerns for such phenomena as acid rain and species extinction. And while there was, no doubt, the occasional climate disaster, rising sea levels and increasingly irregular climate patterns were not on the agendas of cultural leaders. In many ways, it was an idyllic time from the perspective of real and potential ecological emergencies. So the fact that, in the writings of the early church, we do not find debates on these modern calamities should not lull us into thinking that the early church had nothing to say about human stewardship—the care of and respect for God's creation. It was, rather, a recurring theme of their work.

While our attention is often brought to environmental sustainability because of the different crises we face, the early church's love for creation grew out of its love and respect for its Creator. Christians inherited from their Jewish forebears a recognition that the world God created was one that God had judged not just to be good, but to be very good. We see this in the earliest versions of the Creation story from Genesis 1 as well as various places within other books (for example, the Psalms). In each, God's affirmation of the inherent goodness of creation is expressed. From Jewish and biblical roots the early church picked up the importance of care of and respect for creation, and they expressed it often. For a thorough examination of citations throughout church history dealing with care and stewardship of God's creation, consider Fred Krueger's *A Cloud of Witnesses: The Deep Ecological Legacy of Christianity.*[3]

Clement of Rome, called the first of the apostolic fathers, was born in the mid 30s and died in 101. He was one of the earliest popes of the church, having been selected by the Apostle Peter as his immediate successor. What makes Clement of Rome[4] particularly important for our study is that his writings show that explicit respect for God's created order goes all the way back to the earliest times in church history. In his letter to the Corinthians, he describes a universe at peace and in harmony with its Creator. This both honored and pointed to that Creator:

> By his order the heavens moving in the world obey him day and night, they perform the movement determined for them. . . . The sun and the stars shine following in harmony the ways determined by Him without deviation. . . . The unlimited sea, by his will united in great water masses, does not go beyond the limits established by him. . . . The ocean impenetrable for man, the worlds behind it, are administered by the same orders of God. The seasons—spring, summer, autumn and winter—peacefully replace each other. The winds determined for each season, perform their ministry without obstacles. The inexhaustible sources created for delight and health, provide water necessary for human life.[5]

Here, Clement hints at Paul's writings in the early part of the book of Romans. Creation, by its orderliness and consistency, he claimed, made the reality of its Creator obvious to all. Irenaeus picks up a similar theme, making more explicit God's self-revelation through his handiwork:

> That God is the Creator of the world is accepted even by those very persons who in many ways speak against Him, and yet acknowledge Him, styling Him the Creator . . . while the very heathen learned it from the creation itself. For even creation reveals Him who formed it, and the very work made suggests Him who made it, and the world manifests Him who ordered it. The universal Church, moreover, through the whole world, has received this tradition from the apostles themselves.[6]

An important part of the church's respect for God's creation is its recognition that God himself is revealed through it. This idea is picked up frequently.

Clement of Alexandria, a second Clement from the early church, wrote on both theology and the implications for daily life. Krueger writes, "He was the first of Christ's disciples to formulate a theology of lifestyle and shape it into a body of practical doctrine with disciplines for daily activity."[7] He lived from 150 to 215 and, as his name implies, did the bulk of his work in Alexandria. He was born to a well-to-do, but apparently pagan, father and mother. His works indicate that he was a person who had benefited from the classical education of the day and was comfortable quoting Greek philosophers and poets alike. Interestingly, he was a teacher to Origen when he was a student in Alexandria, and Origen took over for him when Clement retired from the Catechetical School. Reading through Clement's writings, one finds an advocate for vegetarianism. In fact, he claims that several of his predecessors, including a few of the disciples of Jesus, were also vegetarians. Overall, Clement argued that the follower of Jesus should live in such a way that embodies simplicity, self-restraint, and constant thankfulness toward God. Let's begin our look at this Clement by considering some of his "lifestyle instructions."

In his work *Christ the Educator*, Clement goes into some detail on "passages from Scripture that bear on education in the practical needs of life and describe the sort of life he who is called a Christian should live throughout his life. We should begin with ourselves, and with the way we should regulate [our actions]."[8] Because much of our potential contemporary ecological crisis is related to our appetites (and the control of our appetites) and because our basic physical need to eat is representative of our most primal appetites, I quote Clement at some length on the issue of food and eating.

Other men, indeed, live that they may eat, just like unreasoning beasts; for them life is only their belly. But as for us, our Educator has given the command that we eat only to live. Eating is not our main occupation, nor is pleasure our chief ambition. . . . Our food should be plain and ungarnished, in keeping with the truth, suitable to children who are plain and unpretentious, adapted to maintaining life, not self-indulgence.

Viewed in this sense, life depends upon two things only: health and strength. To satisfy these needs, all that is required is a disposition easily satisfied with any sort of food; it aids digestion and restricts weight of the body. . . . Surely, excessive variety in food must be avoided, for it gives rise to every kind of bad effect: indisposition of the body, upset stomach, perversion of taste due to some misguided culinary adventure or foolish experiment in pastry cooking. . . . Yet, there are those who grow dissatisfied with the truth in their restless ostentation, and reject simplicity of diet to engage in a frantic search for expensive menus that must be imported from across the sea.

I feel pity for their disease; but they themselves show no shame in flaunting their extravagances, going to no end of trouble to procure lampreys from the Sicilian straits and eels from Maeander, kids from Melos and mullets from Sciathos, Pelordian mussels and Abydean oysters, to say nothing of sprats from Lipara and Mantinean turnips and beets from Ascra. They anxiously search for Methymnian scallops, Attic turgots, laurel-thrushes, and the golden-brown figs for five thousand of which the notorious Persian sent to Greece. On top of all this, they buy fowl from Phasis, francolins from Egypt and peacocks from Medea. Gourmands that they are, they greedily yearn for these fowl and dress them up with sweet sauces, ravenously providing themselves with whatever the land and the depth of sea and the vast expanse of the sky produce as food. Such grasping and excitable people seem to scour the world blunderingly for their costly pleasures, and make themselves heard for their "sizzling frying-pans," wasting the whole of their lives in hovering over mortar and pestle, omnivorous fellows who cling as close to matter as fire does. Why, they deprive even the stable food, bread, of its strength by sifting away the nourishing parts of wheat, turning a necessity of life into a dishonorable pleasure. There is no limit to the gluttony that these men practice. Truly, in ever inventing a multitude of new sweets and ever seeking recipes of every description, they are shipwrecked on pastries and honey-cakes and desserts.

To me, a man of this sort seems nothing more than one great mouth. "Be not desirous," Scripture says, "of the meats of the rich. For those belong to a false and shameful life." These men hug their delicacies to themselves, yet after a while they must yield them to the privy. As for us, who seek a heavenly food, we must restrain the belly and keep it under the control of heaven, and even more that which is made for the belly which "God will destroy," as the Apostle says, intending, no doubt, to curse gluttonous desires. . . .

[Over the next few pages, Clement addresses the manner in which Christians should observe the "love feast" with one another.]

We ought not to misuse the gifts of the Father, then, acting the part of spendthrifts like the rich son in the Gospel; let us, rather, make use of them with detachment, keeping them under control. Surely we have been commanded to be the master and lord, not the slave, of food. It is an admirable thing indeed for a man to depend upon divine food in contemplation of the truth, and to be filled with the vision of that which really is, which is inexhaustible, tasting pleasure

> that is enduring and abiding and pure. Unquestionably, it is contrary to reason, utterly useless, and beneath human dignity for men to feed themselves like cattle being fattened for the slaughter, for those who come from the earth to keep looking down to the earth and ever bowed over their tables. Such men practice a life only of greed, by burying the good of this life in a way that will not last, and paying court only to their bellies, for whose sake they rate cooks more highly than they do those who work the soil.
>
> "It is good," he says, "not to eat meat and not to drink wine," just as the Pythagoreans say. Eating and drinking is the occupation of animals, and the fumes rising from them, heavy and earth-laden, cast a shadow over the soul. But, if anyone partake of them, he does not sin; only let him partake temperately, without being attached to them or dependent upon them, or greedy for any delicacy. A voice will whisper to him: "Do not for the sake of food, destroy the work of God."
>
> Lack of moderation, an evil wherever it is found, is particularly blameworthy in the matter of food. Gourmandising, at least, is nothing more than immoderate use of delicacies; gluttony is a mania for glutting the appetitie, and belly-madness, as the name itself suggests, is lack of self-control with regard to food. . . . If a person is wealthy, yet eats without restraint and shows himself insatiable, he disgraces himself in a special way and does wrong on two scores: first, he adds to the burden of those who do not have, and lays bare, before those who do have, his own lack of temperance.[9]

Clement covers a lot of ground in this section of his work, and it is worth our taking a few mintues to unpack some of the implications.

The overarching point that Clement makes in this passage relates to exercising self-control over our physical desires. For Clement, self-restraint is not something that Christians do "just because." Christians are not to be hedonists or gluttons for very specific reasons: these traits distract us from growing in the image of Christ. By keeping our desires simple, even for basic requirements like food, we maintain our health while avoiding being ruled by our appetites. Clement's concerns are very real and practical for us in the contemporary United States, where many of our major health issues are related to overeating. Common ailments such as diabetes, heart disease, and high blood pressure are all closely connected to obesity. God desires us to find our fulfillment in him. Allowing physical appetites (any of them, even though Clement focuses on food here) to either damage our health or distract us from a growing relationship with God is to misuse that particular blessing. That Clement spends as much time on the issue as he does is noteworthy.

From the third paragraph down, as Clement talks about the desire for exotic foods, I found myself thinking of the plight of the passenger pigeon. In the middle part of the nineteenth century, the number of passenger pigeons in the world was estimated in the billions. However, they were ruthlessly hunted as a food source. At times, the entire body of the bird was discarded in order to harvest the tongue, considered by some to be a delicacy. By the end of 1914, the last passenger pigeon died and the species became extinct. One need not be a vegetarian to see the misuse of creation that results in the extinction of a species. In fact, the rate of the extinction of species has dramatically increased over the course of the last one hundred years.

Clement names many foods that were considered delicacies, prepared in exotic and rich sauces. The principle he argues for, as noted above, is self-restraint. While the principle of self-restraint remains a clear scriptural mandate, today the matter is intensified by the concern that our gluttony is damaging the long-term sustainability of certain food stocks. In our case, then, we have both the need to heed the biblical call to "mortify the flesh" and the challenge of using food sources in a wise and sustainable way—a way that will provide for those in the poorest parts of the world while assuring adequate stores for future generations.

Clement also points out that our gluttony contributes to the suffering of the poor and those whom the Scriptures reference as "the least of these." Specifically, he warns believers not to waste the gifts that God has given, using them like "spendthrifts" rather than good stewards. When we use God's gifts haphazardly, we end up using far more than we need. In the process we deny the poor access to them. Notice that late in the quotation, Clement does not see either the use or the enjoyment of God's creation as evil. We may eat and, of course, there is nothing wrong with enjoying the meals we prepare. He does, however, warn against overconsumption, greed, and allowing our appetites to get the better of us. Likewise, he continually cautions us to keep our desires under control, because allowing them to get the better of us once, makes it easier to fall to them again. In other words, indulging our appetites builds in us a habit of gratification. Vigilance on all matters relating to the satisfying of our appetites and desires is the watchword for Clement. Again, if it was appropriate for Clement to raise these issues in his own context that had none of the ecological crises we face, how much more for us.

Let's consider one more quotation from Clement, this time building on the idea that we ought to use the gift of creation in a sustainable way:

> Those concerned for their salvation should take this as their first principle, that, although the whole of creation is ours to use, the universe is made for the sake of self-sufficiency, which anyone can acquire by a few things. They who rejoice in the holdings in their storehouses are foolish in their greed. "He that hath earned wages," scripture reminds us, "puts them into a bag of holes." Such is the man who gathers and stores up his harvest, for by not sharing his wealth with anyone, he becomes worse off.... To know oneself has always been, so it seems, the greatest of all lessons. For, if anyone knows himself, he will know God; and in knowing God, he will become like Him, not by wearing golden ornaments or by trailing long flowing robes, but by performing good deeds and cultivating an independence of as many things as possible.[10]

Clement observes that the universe is created to be "self-sufficient," which suggests that God's creation is adequate for all our needs. If creation can no longer sustain us, then Clement would suggest that we have allowed our desires to become confused with our needs. Put another way, God's world provides enough for all, but not enough for our insatiable wants and the seemingly irresistible desire to hoard. The world is more than adequate for all to have "enough," but not adequate for some to hoard and utilize the world's resources greedily. "Live simply that others may simply live." These words of Ghandi echo the sentiments we see in Clement.

Marcus Minucius Felix was one of the earliest Christian apologists to write in Latin. Little is known about his life, but he is thought to have died around 250. It seems he was a lawyer who converted to Christian faith in the middle part of his life, though much is less than certain. Krueger writes that "his contribution to a theology of ecology lies in his emphasis upon the Beauty of nature and its ability to lead the soul into appreciation of divinity hidden in all things."[11] Marcus was clear in his statement that God's love extended to all parts of his creation:

> God does not care only for the universe, He also cares for all of its parts. . . . If on entering a house, you should behold everything refined, well arranged and adorned, you would believe that a master presided over it, and that he was much better and above all those excellent things. So in this house of the world, when you look upon the heaven and the earth, its providence, its ordering, its law, believe that there is a Lord and Parent of the universe far more glorious than the stars themselves, and the parts of the whole world.[12]

Not only does Marcus affirm God's care for all of creation, he echoes the belief that creation itself draws attention to its Creator. Both in our call to be imitators of God and in our role as caretakers of the world that God has created, we are called to care for all the parts of creation. We are to tend to them, watch over them, and steward them on God's behalf. When we become irresponsible in our stewardship of creation, the world does not look as orderly. Marcus implies that it looks less like a house in which a "master presided over it." Our own failures to care for creation, in other words, can obscure its normal revelation of its creator.

St. John Chrysostom was a saint and a preacher in the early church, and his name means "golden mouth." We heard from his sermons in Chapter 5. He was quite vocal on issues of wealth and poverty. John was born around 347 in Antioch and died in 407. His father was a ranking military officer and whether his mother was a Christian or not is the subject of debate. His father died, however, shortly after his birth, and subsequently John was raised by his mother. He was well known for his eloquent and articulate preaching, hence the name. John also studied rhetoric and was considered an outstanding public speaker, a skill he used more and more for preaching as his life of faith deepened. Consider a couple of quotations from this preacher. First, just as God's love is over all his creation, so ought our love extend to all of his creatures:

> The saints are exceedingly loving and gentle to mankind, and even to the beasts. . . . Surely we ought to show them great kindness and gentleness for many reasons, but, above all, because they are of the same origin as ourselves.[13]

Note that he begins by observing that kindness to all humans and beasts is a mark of those whom the church has called saint. I wonder if how we treat the animals around us is not an indicator of our overall benevolence. Do we enjoy teasing and exploiting small animals, unable to resist us? It would be interesting to hear what Chrysostom would think of the way we treat some of God's creatures today—particularly those raised in terribly small and miserable conditions simply to be slaughtered as food.

Finally, let's consider one more idea from Chrysostom. Have you ever noticed that Scripture is bracketed by two trees? After the initial creation, when God assigns Adam the task of caring for the garden God has created, the Scriptures explicitly mention the "tree of the knowledge of good and evil" that God has planted in the center of the garden. A little later, the tree of life is mentioned. The failure to observe God's command not to eat from the tree of the knowledge of good and evil brought judgment on all of the created order. At the end of the Scriptures, the tree of life appears again in the renewed heaven and earth, planted in the midst of the new city of God. While he only speaks here of creation, these trees did not escape Chrysostom's attention:

> The tree of life was in the midst of Paradise as a reward; the tree of knowledge as an object of contest and struggle. Having kept the commandment regarding this tree, you will receive a reward. And behold the wondrous thing. Everywhere in Paradise every kind of tree blossoms, everywhere they are abundant in fruit; only in the center are there two trees as an object of battle and exercise.[14]

There is an earthiness to the Scriptures that we often overlook. Trees, gardens, and all manner of living creatures appear within the biblical stories and serve as a setting for the great drama of the history of God and humanity. Unfortunately today, it is too often the case that the created order serves as little more than something to be exploited. The early church knew better and was ever vigilant to warn us not to allow that mood to prevail.

We cannot look into the writings of the early church in an effort to find direct references to what should be done in the face of environmental crises of the magnitude faced in the twenty-first century. These challenges simply did not exist then. We can, however, look at how the early church understood and talked about God's creation. From those writings, we can begin to develop a "theology of creation," and that will help us in a more indirect fashion to respond to current crises. Consider these themes:

1. The early church believed creation revealed God to us,
2. The biblical command encourages us to exercise restraint, and
3. God's love extends to all parts of the created order.

Let us consider each. First, many of the early church writers commented on the orderliness of creation and how it served to draw our attention to its Creator. Yet, God has assigned to humans the task of tending to and overseeing creation. What happens when we do that job badly? What happens when we allow our own selfishness to create ecological problems? In short, creation's reflection of its Creator becomes much less clear, leading to questions about the Creator rather than a recognition that these problems arise from our failures as those charged to care for creation. Does the world have a benevolent creator? If so, did this creator do a shoddy job in creating this world? By failing to do our job to steward creation, we obscure the creation's ability to point beyond itself to God. Just as a messily kept house raises questions about the master or mistress of the house, so our failures to tend to creation properly can inadvertently raise questions about its creator.

Given that so much of the ecological challenge we face is related to habits of consumption, early church reminders of the biblical call to "mortify the flesh" are some of the most salient points to hear. I recall a discussion with a friend who had just returned to the United States after serving outside the country for several years. He commented that what he noticed most was "how much stuff" people seemed to have accumulated while he was gone. In fact, he said he could see a remarkable growth from what he had experienced just five years earlier. While the passages we examined from Clement focused on eating, the comments he made serve as a metaphor for our appetites in general. Building bigger houses means deeper exploitation of building resources; living in bigger houses means more energy consumption; new cars, again, mean more exploitation of natural resources used to build cars; bigger cars, as with bigger houses, mean higher energy usage; higher consumption means further overtaxing our ability to safely deal with all the garbage.

Rodney Clapp observed that all evidence points to the reality that, no matter how much "stuff" we have, we will always want more. Bigger incomes mean bigger houses, newer cars, and not very much more by way of giving to what the Scriptures call "the least of these." Very much of what we as Christians need to do to relieve our obligation to steward the earth would be accomplished if we simply exercised the biblical commands to self-restraint.

Finally, the early church frequently reminds us that God's love surrounds every aspect of creation. As those called to be imitators of God, surely we as Christians should also love every aspect of creation—not just love it in an abstract sense, but rather love it so deeply that we are constantly on the lookout for ways to live better into our stewardship responsibilities. What would it mean to see the world as God sees it? What would it mean to exercise the kind of love God does toward the smallest creature—to the point that he notices every sparrow's death? What it would almost certainly mean is a deliverance from a mentality of exploitation to one of wonder and awe. Once again, the beauty of creation, the subtle ways in which the order inherent in creation gets played out, and the discovery of its breathtaking complexity would serve for us as pointers to the one who created it.

There is a sense in which many of the other chapters of this book are implicated in this one. Our discussions on freedom focused not on the freedom to consume and exploit, but rather on freedom from sin—a close parallel to Clement's words about self-control and restraint. Our discussions on wealth and poverty get at the proper use of blessings—blessings that often take a very physical form. Greed both prevents care for the least of these and exercises what Clement called a "spendthrift's" attitude toward the world. It is hard to imagine anything with more actual and potential damage to the earth than war, which makes our calling to be peacemakers particularly striking. How we conceive of empires and nation-states and what privileges and rights they possess affects how we think of stewardship of the world. If we think the state exists just to fuel our liberty to do as we please with minimal constraints, then we are likely to judge ourselves to have the right to exploit the created order in any way we desire. Themes of the right use of creation run through almost everything else we do. May God open our eyes to this reality, and may God bless us with the ability to see the beauty and grandeur of the world as God does!

Part Three: Civil Life

VII. Society and Government

Stan Hauerwas once commented that, in the West today, we are all liberals. Now, lest liberal readers start nodding their heads in satisfaction, he was not offering a compliment. And, before conservative readers start nodding their heads in satisfaction at that, we must note that he was not using the term *liberal* in the popular sense. For example, he did not mean that we are all *theological liberals*, for indeed we are not. In similar fashion, he did not mean that we are all *political liberals*, for of course, we are not all political liberals either (if by that we meant liberal on certain economic and social issues as opposed to being conservative on the same set of issues). No, what he meant was that we are all liberal in that we take utterly for granted the rightness of the modern liberal democratic project. But, that still leaves things too unclear. Let me say a bit more about what all this means.

John Locke is generally considered the one who first gave articulation to this sense of liberalism and to liberal democracy as a form of government. He defended his vision based on the concept of "natural rights" and believed that representative forms of government exist primarily to protect life, liberty, and property. Liberalism embraced the fundamental equality of all, leading to voting systems that assured that the "will of the public" could be tested, and then implemented. This form of government has largely become the standard in the contemporary West and seems to be increasingly popular in areas that have traditionally resisted it.

A key component of liberal democracy, or Lockean liberalism, is the segregation of the world into two "realms." There is a public realm where arguments are to be won and policy decisions are to be made on the basis of rationality with the goal of maximizing everyone's personal liberty. Then, there is the private sphere, the personal space of every individual, where persons are allowed to believe as they choose. A person's religious commitments go in the private sphere. The liberal democratic tradition both assigns religion to the private realm and attempts thereby to protect it from meddling by the state. When we consider the matter from Locke's historical perspective, it is not hard to understand his privatization of religious faith. He was well aware of our history of wars and conflicts rooted in religious differences between nations and often within nations. Similarly, one can hardly criticize the goals he had in mind. By moving expressions of religious faith to the "private sphere"[1] and by attempting to keep the "public sphere" free from religion, he believed he was accomplishing two goods. First, he believed that he was protecting the freedom of religious expression. By not having an official state religion, each and every person was free to exercise faith in whatever way she or he thought appropriate. The state could only step in, according to Locke, when there was risk of harm to someone. For example, if a religion attempted to practice human sacrifice, the state could intervene to protect life. However, virtually all other religious expressions were to be left to each individual and/or group of individuals to determine for themselves. Second, he thought he was protecting the state from becoming overly connected with one religious tradition. For example, Locke suggests no connection between citizenship and membership in a particular faith group. No one can be penalized for being a member of a minority faith group, nor can anyone be required to participate in any particular form of religious observance. One might even choose to be an atheist. By making this separation, he believed he had found a way around repeating the history of religious wars. Again, one cannot fault him for these two goals, but as is often the case, the problems come from the more-or-less unintended consequences of the move to separate church and state in this way.

Now, it is important to note that the normal partisan distinctions that we make—dividing ourselves up into Democrats and Republicans, perhaps adding in the Green and Libertarian parties on occasion—are not particularly important. Liberal democracy, embodied in a representative republic, is the fundamental assumption driving the vast majority of virtually all major parties. The issue we are addressing is not a partisan issue, but rather an attempt to challenge the underlying presuppositions of Lockean liberalism or democratic liberalism. What we are attempting to ask ourselves here is whether *those assumptions themselves* are problematic from a Christian perspective. And, in due course, we will look back to the earliest church period to see what wisdom we can gain.

Critics of Lockean liberalism object on a number of points. First, because of the focus on private religious expression and the right of all to practice religion as each sees fit, Lockean liberalism involves an unwitting tendency to make religion seem little more than a matter of individual choice. Christian faith is a deeply communal practice, but the view of religion embedded in liberal democracy invites an overly high degree of individualism, with the freedom to pursue one's desires as the highest good. In the process, liberal democracy assumes that we can live rightly together by establishing the "right" laws rather than by developing the inherent trust required in a more communally oriented way of life. In the long run, as Hauerwas has argued,[2] Lockean liberalism undermines the ability to build the very sort of communities it claims to support. As it turns out, an approach that depends primarily on rules to govern our behavior has been an inadequate substitute for the trust that is built between persons as they share in community together.

Second and more importantly, by making religion a private matter, Lockean liberalism takes away one of the critical moral underpinnings of society.[3] Religious traditions, operating in private, fail to exert an adequate public influence on the formation of character. In fact, when religious folks argue for broad application of particular moral behaviors, those in the public sphere often criticize the religious. Why? Because they believe that in so doing religion oversteps its proper bounds. Even worse, we Christians often end up distinguishing between behaviors that are expected "in church" and those that are expected "in public." We cannot be expected, so the argument goes, to treat everyone the way we are to treat Christian sisters and brothers. And so, even within the church we often see private and public morality as different things. Then, of course, one has to ask what counts as moral training in our liberal democracies where the primary focus is on maximizing personal liberty so that each person is free to do as he or she sees best.[4] In essence, the moral failings of liberal democracies are often made worse by the absence of a religious tradition that knows to challenge the seeming rightness of everyone having the liberty to do as they please. We have forgotten the importance of virtue and the role of the religious community in the formation of virtuous persons. Perhaps even more important, we have lost the critical importance of controlling our desires rather than merely aiming to maximize personal liberty.

Third, and closely related to the second point, by declaring liberty the end goal of human existence, Lockean liberalism undermines a more biblical view of our life's purpose. As Hauerwas writes, "People feel their only public duty is to follow their own interests as far as possible, limited only by the rule that we do not unfairly limit others' freedom."[5] But, can this really be the end goal for which God created us? The freedom to pursue our own desires? What do we do with biblical claims that we are to restrain and even "mortify" our desires for possessions, glory, and power? Lockean liberalism assumes that we can build a just society on little more than competing self-interests and laws that will maximize liberty for all. It may not be a surprise, then, that Lockean liberal democracy "becomes a self-fulfilling prophecy; a social order that is designed to work on the presumption that people are self-interested tends to produce that kind of people."[6] In short, by privatizing religion, liberal democracy turned its back on the formation of a character that embraced self-restraint, sacrifice, and the biblical command to put the interests of others above our own. Instead, it offered a new morality that turned the old morality on its head by making virtues the very things the Christian tradition had seen as vices: self-interest and the desire to acquire things. Those traits that had long been held as vices were now virtues that were intended to realize the assumed goal of human existence—the maximization of personal liberty to do as one pleases.[7]

We have spent much time on developing these points because, to be honest, I suspect this sounds very strange to contemporary ears. We take the presuppositions of liberal democracy utterly for granted in our society and, perhaps more amazingly, within our churches. I have even seen folks attempt to build a case for why the modern liberal democratic state is exactly what God has in mind for us. Perhaps we should question some of these presuppositions, particularly in light of their effects. Many of our public institutions are in shambles, exploitation by clever marketing schemes has led to a housing collapse, and we have a surprisingly hard time putting moral language to the injustices of income inequality. On what grounds, exactly, do we complain when individual liberty and the pursuit of self-interest are the norm for the day? Yet, something is wrong. As Hauerwas puts it, "A polity is ultimately judged by the kind of people it produces, and from such a perspective our society can only be found wanting."[8] While liberal democracy has been the norm for a few hundred years, it was not always the case. Let's take a look at how the early church understood its connections to the empire/state.

We all know of the persecutions of the early church. To say that the Roman Empire was hostile to Christian faith would be a bit of an understatement. While the persecution was not constant, it was frequent in the period prior to Constantine, that is, up until the early 300s. As reported earlier, the fathers of both Origen and Ambrose had been martyred during outbreaks of persecution. Sometimes the persecution was a more local phenomenon; other times it was empire-wide and undertaken at the order of the imperial court. Simply for being Christians, persons were beaten, flogged, burned at the stake, or fed to the lions in the Colosseum. Church historians identify ten distinct periods of persecution, beginning with Nero in the middle 60s and ending with Diocletian in the early 300s. The last persecution the worst of all. Clearly, during this time there was no easy alliance between Christian faith and the empire. However, while one might expect that new conversions to Christianity would be dampened by these bouts of persecution, quite the opposite was the case. The church seemed always to grow faster during periods of persecution. It was the early Latin church father Tertullian who was first reported as saying, "The blood of the martyrs is the seed of the church."[9]

Perhaps the words of the martyrs served to cause those listening to reconsider the faith. Certainly, we have many accounts of their words as they were on their way to death. Consider Ignatius:

> May I enjoy the wild beasts that are prepared for me; and I pray that they may be found eager to rush upon me, which also I will entice to devour me speedily, and not deal with me as with some, whom, out of fear, they have not touched. But if they be unwilling to assail me, I will compel them to do so. Pardon me [in this] I know what is for my benefit. Now I begin to be a disciple, and have no desire after anything visible or invisible, that I may attain to Jesus Christ. Let fire and the cross; let the crowds of wild beasts; let breakings, tearings, and separations of bones; let cutting off of members; let bruising to pieces of the whole body; and let the very torment of the devil come upon me: only let me attain to Jesus Christ.[10]

Or, when Polycarp, who was a disciple of the Apostle John, was asked at the age of eighty-six to deny Christ, he responded:

> Fourscore and six years have I been serving him, and he hath done me no wrong; how then can I blaspheme my king who saved me?[11]

A little later, Polycarp was offered deliverance if he would swear by the emperor's genius.[12]

> If thou vainly supposest that I will swear by the genius of Caesar, as thou sayest, feigning to be ignorant who I am, hear plainly: I am a Christian. But if thou desirest to learn the doctrine of Christianity, assign a day and hear.[13]

We could go on with additional examples, but the point would be the same. When persecution of Christians broke out in the empire, we find courageous women and men who stood ready to die before surrendering their faith or compromising it with allegiance to the emperor. In the case of Polycarp, he was tied to the stake to be burned, but when the flames did not kill him, a soldier stepped forward and stabbed him with a sword. One has to wonder, though, why this persecution? Why did the empire feel such a need to stamp out the Christian faith in such horrible ways? What threat could Polycarp have been as an eighty-six-year-old man?

When the Roman Empire was overrun in 410, there were many who blamed Christians for the collapse of the state. The charge cast at Christians, as odd as it sounds to our ears, is that they were atheists. Roman mythology had its pantheon of gods, and the true believers, so they thought, were persons who believed in the gods of that pantheon. Christians, because they worshiped a different God, were considered by the Romans to be unbelievers—atheists. Those who blamed Christians for the fall of Rome believed that Christians had upset the Roman gods, causing them to withdraw their protection and to allow the defeat of the empire. How had Christians upset the Roman gods? By refusing to acknowledge their existence. In so doing, Christians did not show proper piety to the gods and, consequently, offended them. In the third century, a Roman philosopher named Porphyry wrote:

> How can people not be in every way impious and atheistic who have apostatized from the customs of our ancestors through which every nation and city is sustained? . . . What else are they than fighters against God?[14]

Notice the close connection between religion and the good of the nation. The religious of Rome observed the religious traditions of their ancestors and they did so because they believed this would assure protection of the empire.

To the contemporary religious observance of Rome, during the early church period, the focus was on utility—that is, how religious practice served the city/empire. This would have seemed quite upside down to the early church. According to Roman religion, the attitude one was to hold toward the gods was one characterized as piety. But, as Robert Wilkin notes, it was not the personal piety that we think of today that they had in mind. Instead, there was a very tight set of connections between civic and religious duties with both having the same end: the well-being of the commonwealth. He goes on to describe this in more detail:

> In the cities of the Roman Empire, religion was inextricably intertwined with social and political life. Piety toward the gods was thought to insure the wellbeing of the city, to promote a spirit of kinship and mutual responsibility, to bind together the citizenry. "In all probability," wrote Cicero, "disappearance of piety toward the gods will entail the disappearance of loyalty and social union among men as well, and of justice itself, the queen of all the virtues." In the most profound sense, then, impiety toward the gods disrupted society, and when piety disappears, said Cicero, "life soon becomes a welter of disorder and confusion."[15]

Since Christians tended to stay to themselves, worshiping in privacy and not intruding on public occasions, why were they perceived to be impious? The early Romans accused Christians of not only lacking piety, they also labeled them as superstitious:

> In his letter Pliny calls Christianity a "degenerate sort of cult carried to extravagant lengths." The term he uses for a degenerate cult is *superstitio*. (This same word is used by two contemporaries, the historians Tacitus and Suetonius, to designate Christianity. Tacitus terms Christianity a "deadly superstition," and Suetonius calls Christians a "class of persons given to a new and mischievous superstition.")[16]

Christians constituted a degenerate cult because they did not participate in the same rituals of worship and community life as the Roman citizens. Add to that the way they spoke of the Lord's Supper (eating the flesh of Christ), and you can see why folks were a bit squeamish about Christians. These superstitious folk, then, did not serve the empire, and in fact undermined it through their failure to be assimilated into Roman religion:

> To say that a group was "superstitious" meant that its rites and customs set the people apart from the rest of society. The superstitious did not conform their lives to the traditions of most citizens. They were "other," just as the saffron-robed Hare Krishna monks are to most Americans. Their otherness was, however, not simply social; it was also religious. What set them apart were not only national customs and familial traditions but also religious rituals and beliefs. In saying that Christians were "superstitious," the Romans were making a religious judgment about their way of life.[17]

One reason for the persecution of Christians was that they were judged to be hostile to the Roman pantheon. In turn, the pantheon was very tightly coupled with the existence of Roman cities and the empire itself. Christians were judged hostile because they saw the Roman gods as idols and because they did not participate in the customs handed down from previous generations. Christians had their own developing traditions and they worshiped together with those like-minded. This gave the appearance of a cult of "outsiders." In setting themselves apart from the state rather than setting themselves up as partners with the state, they declared allegiance to a different world—a world beyond this physical one, and certainly not the one known as the Roman Empire. In short, Romans believed the purpose of religion was to unite the empire, and the conduct and beliefs of Christianity did not serve this model. Its rituals, sabbaths, and feasts were conducted with congregations of believers, not in the public sphere. The differing religions, then, observed different polities, and Christians were seen as a threat to the normal unity-building nature of Roman religion. Roman religion was good and effective as long as it had the outcomes desired—public unity, public piety, and safety for the commonwealth. Christian practice undermined that, and the Romans felt they had little option but to force Christians to convert—at least partway. Once the Christians resisted, persecutions often followed.

It has been observed that, as a general rule, the Romans were quite tolerant of other religions. But that tolerance, too, could only go as far as it served the health of the empire. The tendency of Christians to create their own communities and to see themselves as "resident aliens" in this world could hardly endear them to the defenders of the empire. It was not that Christians were openly hostile to the emperor, but rather that they were not particularly accommodating. They felt they were simply being faithful to the command to have no God above the God and Father of our Lord Jesus. They intended no specific disrespect for Caesar, but they were equally concerned that they treat Caesar as was due a human, albeit a human ruling the civil government. Consider Tertullian:

> But why dwell longer on the reverence and sacred respect of Christians to the emperor, whom we cannot but look up to as called by our Lord to his office? So that on valid grounds I might say Caesar is more ours than yours, for our God has appointed him. Therefore, as having this propriety in him, I do more than you for his welfare, not merely because I ask it of Him who can give it, or because I ask it as one who deserves to get it, but also because, in keeping the majesty of Caesar within due limits, and putting it under the Most High, and making it less than divine, I commend him the more to the favour of Deity, to whom I make him alone inferior. But I place him in subjection to one I regard as more glorious than himself. Never will I call the emperor God, and that either because

> it is not in me to be guilty of falsehood; or that I dare not turn him into ridicule; or that not even himself will desire to have that high name applied to him. If he is but a man, it is his interest as man to give God His higher place. Let him think it enough to bear the name of emperor. That, too, is a great name of God's giving. To call him God, is to rob him of his title. If he is not a man, emperor he cannot be. Even when, amid the honours of a triumph, he sits on that lofty chariot, he is reminded that he is only human. A voice at his back keeps whispering in his ear, "Look behind thee; remember thou art but a man."[18]

Tertullian notes that Christians pray for the emperor and wish the best for him as one called to his place by God. Tertullian notes, however, that Christians serve Caesar well precisely because they do not regard him as divine. There is but one God, and to pretend Caesar, a human, is divine would be to traffic in lies and falsehood, Tertullian argues. Christians could not allow themselves to accept the Roman pantheon, including the emperor's claims to deity. So, they became, according to Romans, atheists and unbelievers, a crass and uneducated people, who did not rightly understand the role of the empire.

Justin Martyr recognizes similar points when he says Christians are quite happy to follow Roman rule at any point that does not conflict with God's commands, particularly around worship:

> Whence to God alone we render worship, but in other things we gladly serve you, acknowledging you as kings and rulers of men, and praying that with your kingly power you be found to possess also sound judgment. But if you pay no regard to our prayers and frank explanations, we shall suffer no loss, since we believe (or rather, indeed, are persuaded) that every man will suffer punishment in

> eternal fire according to the merit of his deed, and will render account according to the power he has received from God, as Christ intimated when He said, "To whom God has given more, of him shall more be required."[19]

We Christians will gladly obey the emperor, but not when his demands create a conflict with those things due only to the Christian God—worship, love, allegiance. We must not underestimate the extent to which this was seen as sacrilege by the Romans, particularly the emperor. One of the ordering principles of the empire was the identity, and even deity, of Caesar. Christians could not swear allegiance to the emperor, for as aliens of another land, merely taking temporary resident status "here," Christians were obliged to reject any form of idolatry. To go with the crowd in affirming the deity of the emperor would have been to participate in idolatry.

Further in his apology, Tertullian makes explicit his concerns:

> This is the reason, then, why Christians are counted public enemies: that they pay no vain, nor false, nor foolish honours to the emperor; that, as men believing in the true religion, they prefer to celebrate their festal days with a good conscience, instead of with the common wantonness. It is, forsooth, a notable homage to bring fires and couches out before the public, to have feasting from street to street, to turn the city into one great tavern, to make mud with wine, to run in troops to acts of violence, to deeds of shamelessness to lust allurements! What! is public joy manifested by public disgrace? Do things unseemly at other times beseem the festal days of princes? Do they who observe the rules of virtue out of reverence for Caesar, for his sake turn aside from them? Shall piety be a license to immoral deeds, and shall religion be regarded as affording the occasion for all riotous extravagance? Poor

> we, worthy of all condemnation! For why do we keep the votive days and high rejoicings in honour of the Caesars with chastity, sobriety, and virtue? Why, on the day of gladness, do we neither cover our door-posts with laurels, nor intrude upon the day with lamps? It is a proper thing, at the call of a public festivity, to dress your house up like some new brothel. However, in the matter of this homage to a lesser majesty, in reference to which we are accused of a lower sacrilege, because we do not celebrate along with you the holidays of the Caesars in a manner forbidden alike by modesty, decency, and purity,—in truth they have been established rather as affording opportunities for licentiousness than from any worthy motive;—in this matter I am anxious to point out how faithful and true *you* are, lest perchance here also those who will not have us counted Romans, but enemies of Rome's chief rulers, be found themselves worse than we wicked Christians.[20]

Summarizing, why were Christians seen as atheists and troublemakers? First, they did not observe the Roman pantheon and, explicitly, they were unwilling to concede the claim that the emperor was divine. Thus, they were unwilling to supplant their own affirmation, "Jesus is Lord" with "Caesar is Lord." In this way, they refused to share in a significant and common element of the empire's theo-politics.[21] Second, Tertullian notes why Christians are unwilling to participate in the city's festivals: they became little more than license to immoral behavior. Perhaps the city's rituals were "community building," but according to Tertullian, Christians could not participate because of the licentiousness. Again, Christians set themselves apart, a different society with a different politic. For this "otherness," they often suffered persecution at the hands of the Romans.

Connecting the threads together shows that the church has not always taken the ideals and practices of "Lockean liberalism" as normative for how they are to behave with regard to the empire or nation-state. During its early period, the church was willing to "be the church" and had no interest in avoiding their existence as "resident aliens" in the empire. They did not feel particularly inclined to defend the existence of the empire or the emperor, though they were not particularly opposed to them either. As we will see in a subsequent chapter, when asked to take up arms in support of the empire, those in the earliest period of the church almost uniformly declined. More cognizant of their status as resident aliens, a people whose citizenship and allegiance were not with Rome, they were happy to stay focused on the advancement of God's reign in the world. They focused first and foremost to model God's reign in their own devotion to their Lord. When threatened with persecution for failing to show proper deference to the emperor, they counted it an honor to be a martyr for the cause of Christ. There could be no compromise on the affirmation: Jesus is Lord.

All of this changed substantially in 313, when the rulers of the eastern and western halves of the Roman Empire (Licinius and Constantine, respectively) signed the Edict of Milan. This edict established religious tolerance within the empire. For Licinius, a pagan, it really meant little more than toleration; but for Constantine, already a Christian, it meant the active promotion and support of the Christian faith. Rather than being outsiders to the halls of power, Christians now found themselves not only welcomed but favored. As with many things, the so-called Constantinian settlement has been judged both a great and a terrible thing. On one side, scholars affirm the cessation of persecution, the normalization of religious life, and the welcoming of the religious voice in the workings of the empire. On the other side, scholars have expressed concern over the church losing sight of its status as resident aliens, the compromise required now to appease its new imperial partner, and the ease with which the church could wield power with no less harshness than pagans. Some see the Edict of Milan as a great step forward for the church while others have characterized it as "the Constantinian fall." Perhaps, as is so often the case, there is truth to both claims. Even so, we must be careful not to miss the path that was set for the church at this point and the extent to which the Edict of Milan invited the church to become the chaplains to the empire and later to the nation-state. To see how close the thought embodied in the Edict was to that of the Roman utilitarian view of religion noted above, consider these words from it:

> Wherefore, for this our indulgence, they ought to pray to their God for our safety, for that of the republic, and for their own, that the commonwealth may continue uninjured on every side, and that they may be able to live securely in their homes.[22]

In exchange for toleration, the Edict says, the religious ought to be concerned about the empire, support it, and pray to their God for it. Many have said Constantine was brilliant for co-opting the church in this way. And, who could blame Christians for taking advantage of it? The Diocletian persecution had just ended. A respite from persecution and the offer of a better relation with the empire were irresistible.

But, with partnership comes a change in perspective, a certain loss of the ability to speak prophetically. After Constantine, the church's role has oft been described as "chaplain" to the empire. As Michael Budde and Robert Brimlow note in *Christianity Incorporated,*[23] chaplains exist to comfort the afflicted, offer the appropriate rituals over state functions, and to offer moral support. They are not allowed, however, to challenge the fundamental presuppositions of the institution to which they serve as chaplain. In accepting a place at Constantine's table, the church would be forever changed, now a partner with a vested interest in empire, now a chaplain for whom it would be rude and unacceptable to challenge the very foundations of empire. In so doing, the church surrendered an important part of its role as moral influence in the empire. Its critique of the imperial court had to be attenuated, had to be made more hearable to imperial ears. Did the early church gain more or lose more from this compromise with empire, with Constantine?

In Lockean liberalism, the church accepts a distinction between the public and the private in exchange for the freedom to worship as it chooses in private. The exchange is hardly ever spoken of as an exchange, but what the church lost in the exchange was a not so subtle change in its understanding of liberty.[24] Religious toleration in private meant the acceptance of the societal goal of the maximization of personal liberty and the willingness largely to turn a blind eye to the Christian faith's critique of our sinful appetites. Greed is hardly challenged, because to speak of greed is to make a judgment about another's personal liberty. Gluttony is similarly off the table.

In other words, the church has implicitly agreed, for the most part, to mute or render vague and abstract its prophetic voice on the impropriety of the right for everyone to do "what they think to be right." Such liberty is now judged a virtue rather than a vice. We in the church rarely offer meaningful challenge to the underlying presuppositions of liberal democracy. In fact, we most often accept them as consistent with biblical values. With Constantine, the exchange was both similar and different. It was similar in that the exchange was a muting of the church's prophetic voice against its new partner, the empire. In other words, the church mostly avoided challenges to the underlying presuppositions of empire, often now instead defending them. The difference was, primarily, that the structures that channeled power were different.

In either case, the church engages in a fundamental shift when for safety and security within the empire it trades its ability to "be the church" and its ability to model a different way of being in the world, a way characterized by the phrase "resident aliens." When the church gives up being the church, it removes from society one of its most important gifts—a reminder that there is a different way, there is an alternative way of being, a way more consistent with the end God has in mind for us. May we, in the church, look back to the earliest period of our Christian forebears and consider how we might recover the deep sense of allegiance they had to a different king and a different polity. Then, may we once again become both a light to the world and the embodiment of an oasis where God's reign is already active and alive, ready to infiltrate and undermine all other ways of being!

VIII.

The Early Church on War

Over the centuries, Christians have held different positions on the best way to think about war and Christian participation in war. There was the period of the Crusades when war was seen as a holy cause, largely targeting the recovery of holy lands that had been captured by the Muslims. While no longer argued explicitly along the lines of crusades, some modern positions are clearly indebted to the crusade mentality. I will refer to those who hold this position as "Crusaders." From at least the time of Augustine (that is, from the fourth and fifth centuries), many Christians have held that Christians may only participate in war if it is "just." Those who hold this position I will reference as "just war theorists" or "JWTs." Augustine began the Christian discussion of what set of conditions would, together, make a particular war justified, making it acceptable for Christians to participate. In the Middle Ages, St. Thomas Aquinas expanded Augustine's thinking. There is no doubt but that the vast majority of Christians today would classify themselves as supporters of the just war theory. Finally, there has always been a strand of the Christian faith that holds that war is never justified, and therefore, that it is never acceptable for a Christian to participate in war.

Some who hold this position find that the conditions laid out by just war theory can never be met (and so, according to them, there could never be a just war). Others hold that obedience to the Lord will not allow participation in war, just or not. I will reference those who follow this position as Christian pacifists.

As one might expect, there are significant differences even within each of the three positions. For example, John Howard Yoder, one of the more significant advocates of Christian pacifism in the last one hundred years, wrote a book called *Nevertheless.* In it, he outlined over twenty different versions of Christian pacifism. Similarly, JWTs differ on exactly what set of conditions render a war just or whether all or some subset of the conditions have to be met to justify a particular war. Further, over time, JWTs have argued that the conditions that justify war have to be changed, in light of technological developments, for example. It is easier, then, to analyze a *tradition of just war thinking* rather than a static just war theory. While the Crusader position is much less frequently proposed or defended explicitly, if we were to dig into the details, we would find differences there as well. Are crusades always religious in nature, and if so, how do incipient religious conflicts become full-fledged holy wars? These subtle nuances, however, are not necessary for our study of the early church's position on war.

As noted above, a wide majority of contemporary Christians would embrace some version of the just war theory; that is, they would argue that Christians can participate in war as long as the war meets certain criteria. We have already learned something about the life of Augustine in an earlier chapter. In addition to being a great defender of Christian faith and doctrine, he is often credited as the founder of Christian just war thinking. There are three preliminary points to address in Augustine's writings on Christians and war (one of which we will supplement with the later work of Aquinas). First, the timing of his work is important. Chapter 7 noted that Christian attitudes toward empire changed during the time of Constantine. The changes more closely aligned Christian faith with the empire. After the Edict of Milan, Christians had a vested interest in the defense of the empire. The Edict was issued in 313, and Augustine was not born until 354. Augustine's work on the Christian participation in war, then, was all undertaken after this epochal change in the relationship between church and empire. It would not be surprising, then, to find a difference in the Christian position on war before and after Constantine, and, thus, to find differences between Augustine and those from earlier in church history.

Second, given the extent to which Augustine is cited as the father of Christian just war theory, we might expect to find a specific and systematic treatment of the subject in his writings. This is not the case. Augustine's comments on just war are scattered and relatively few, with the most significant appearing in *The City of God.* Even here, Augustine's insights occur largely within just a few passages. It is noteworthy that Augustine found the proper *personal* Christian response to aggression to be pacifism. He did not make a case for an individual right of self-defense. Under certain conditions, which Augustine argued had to be rooted in Christian love and which were largely characterized under the rubric of restoring peace, political entities could engage in war and Christians could participate.

Third, Augustine's use of the Scriptures in defense of the just war theory is minimal. This is a bit odd for Augustine, given how he often intersperses his writings with biblical references. He provides some references to the Old Testament and to wars conducted under God's command, but he offers no insights on how the incarnation and life of Jesus affects those.[1]

St. Thomas Aquinas later picks up Augustine's thought and treats the question of just wars in a more systematic fashion. Aquinas begins his inquiry by asking "whether it is always sinful to wage war."[2] Dombrowski calls our attention to the form of the question, in particular the use of the word *always*. Clearly, Dombrowski notes, the presumption is, at least, that one has to justify a given war, and the burden is on the one arguing for war. To ask the question if it is *always wrong* to do X is to imply that it *usually is wrong*. Then, Aquinas goes on to list three biblical passages, two from Jesus and one from Paul. They are: Matthew 26:52 ("All those who use the sword will die by the sword"), Matthew 5:39 ("But I say to you that you must not oppose those who want to hurt you"), and Romans 12:19 ("Don't try to get revenge for yourselves, my dear friends, but leave room for God's wrath"). Aquinas does not take up any of these passages directly. Instead, he cites a sermon where Augustine depends not on Jesus, but rather on John the Baptist:

> If the Christian Religion forbade war altogether, those who sought salutary advice in the Gospel would rather have been counselled to cast aside their arms, and to give up soldiering altogether. On the contrary, they were told: "Do violence to no man . . . and be content with your pay" [Luke 3:14]. If he commanded them to be content with their pay, he did not forbid soldiering.[3]

In other words, Aquinas and Augustine seem to find it decisive that John the Baptist did not tell these persons to leave military service.

From here, Aquinas moves directly to talk about the conditions that make a war just, assuming apparently that he has adequately answered the biblical challenges. Interestingly, however, when Aquinas moves to the question of whether it is lawful for clerics and bishops to fight, he answers this question with a resounding "no," using Matthew 26:52 ("Put the sword back into its place") as his proof text. Why is it that Christians in general may make war, but not priests and bishops? Because, Aquinas says, in this passage Jesus is speaking to Peter as the representative of all clerics and bishops. Why Peter is representative of clerics and bishops and not all Christians is left unanswered. And, we are likewise left uncertain why Aquinas draws the conclusion he does.

It does not mean that just war theory is mistaken because Augustine, and later Aquinas, defended just war after the Constantinian legitimation of Christian faith. It is not necessarily false because they provide no systematic treatment of the question. Nor does a lack of a strong biblical defense of their positions prove it wrong. From time to time, the church has held that certain kinds of issues are not decisively addressed in Scripture. In those cases, the church has held that one must reason carefully and humbly, trusting that God will lead one in the right direction. Perhaps this is the case with just war theory, and we ought not be too quick to dismiss this possibility. Before drawing any conclusions, though, let's take a look at the position of leaders within the church during the period prior to Augustine.

Prior to the year A.D. 200, the early church was overwhelmingly pacifist. In his book *Early Fathers on War and Military Service*, Louis Swift comments that, while he did not want to think the early church was overwhelmingly pacifist, the documentary evidence runs to the contrary. That is an interesting admission to say the least. Between 200 and the Edict of Milan, the church was still predominantly pacifist, but evidence of military participation was increasing. Let's take a look at what many of the early fathers had to say about the topic.

We begin our examination by considering the writings of Tertullian. He was born in Carthage around 160 and lived until approximately 225.[4] While many of the most influential fathers of the period were Greek-speaking easterners, Tertullian was a Latin-speaking westerner. Some consider him the father of Western Christianity. We know relatively little about Tertullian's early life. He seems to have been trained in law, and his writing style seems consistent with that. Whatever comprised his early life he was not converted to Christian faith until near 200 (his first writing in defense of Christianity is from 197). Once converted, though, he became a prolific writer, dealing with a variety of topics. His use of the term *trinity* (*trinitas* in Latin) was the first recorded instance we can find. His expression of the trinitarian doctrine (three persons, one substance) was also very early. Thirty-one of Tertullian's writings survive, along with fragments of several others. While of Latin provenance, as we noted, he also wrote in Greek. His interests were wide ranging, and he wrote on topics all across the Christian spectrum—apologetics, particularly against paganism and heresy, as well as topics that we would call ethics today. With this broad interest, it is not surprising that he addresses the issue of Christian faith and participation in war.

Writing in his *On Idolatry*, Tertullian takes up the question:

> The question also concerning military service, and whether the military—at least the rank and file or all the inferior grades, who are under no necessity of offering sacrifices or passing capital sentences—may be admitted to the faith. There is no congruity between the divine and human "sacramentum," the sign of Christ and the sign of the devil, the camp of light and the camp of darkness: one soul cannot be owed to two, God and Caesar. And yet, some Christians say, Moses carried a rod, and Aaron wore a buckle, and John was girt with a leather belt, and Joshua . . . led a line of march, and the people waged war, if it is your pleasure to sport with the subject. But how will a Christian make war—nay, how will he serve as a soldier in peace time—without a sword, which the Lord hath taken away? For, although soldiers had come to John and received the form of a rule, although also a centurion had believed, yet the Lord afterwards, in disarming Peter, ungirded every soldier. No dress is lawful among us which is assigned to an unlawful practice.[5]

Interesting, is it not, that the passage Augustine and Aquinas thought significant is judged by Tertullian to be inadequate in light of Jesus' subsequent command to put away the sword. Clearly, Tertullian answers the same question Aquinas did. But, for Aquinas, the command to Peter was only to the clergy and ecclesiastical authorities. For Tertullian, it was a statement for all Christians to heed: when the Lord told Peter to put away the sword, according to Tertullian, he was speaking to all followers of Jesus.

In a longer passage, Tertullian raises a number of questions, assuming that the reader will concur with him in his conclusions about war:

> To begin with the real ground of the military crown, I think we must first inquire whether warfare is proper at all for Christians.[6]

The term *military* crown is a reference to the laurel that victors in various contests and battles might wear as an indication of military service to the empire. Later, Tertullian addressed whether the wearing of the crown was idolatrous. But, notice that before he got to that, he took up the question of Christian participation in war more generally. He continues:

> Shall it be held lawful to make an occupation of the sword, when the Lord proclaims that he who uses the sword shall perish by the sword? And shall the son of peace take part in the battle when it does not become him even to sue at law? And shall he apply the chain, and the prison, and the torture, and the punishment, who is not the avenger even of his own wrongs?[7]

Tertullian makes several appeals here. First, we see again the passage noted earlier. For Tertullian, if the Lord has proclaimed that users of the sword die by the sword, then it follows that Christians ought not to use the sword. Next, he reminds us as Christians that we are followers of the Prince of Peace, and thus children of peace ourselves. If the followers of the Prince of Peace are not even to go to court to make things right, how much less can we go to war. Finally, he observes that we are all deserving of punishment for our wrongs and, thus, should not be so quick to visit punishments on the heads of others.

As he moves on through his argument, Tertullian turns his attention to those who become followers of Jesus after they have joined in military service. At first, he observes this is a different case:

> Of course, if faith comes later, and finds any preoccupied with military service, their case is different, as in the instance of those whom John used to receive for baptism, and of those most faithful centurions, I mean the centurion whom Christ approves, and the centurion whom Peter instructs. . . .[8]

But, then with a subtle shift, he goes on to write:

> . . . yet, at the same time, when a man has become a believer, and faith has been sealed, there must be either an immediate abandonment of it, which has been the course with many; or all sorts of quibbling will have to be resorted to in order to avoid offending God, and that is not allowed even outside of military service; or, last of all, for God the fate must be endured which a citizen-faith has been no less ready to accept. Neither does military service hold out escape from punishment of sins, or exemption from martyrdom. Nowhere does the Christian change his character.[9]

Even though Tertullian begins by observing that things are different for one who was a soldier when he became a follower of Jesus, he quickly makes it clear that, as far as he is concerned, there is only one option for such a person. They must abandon war-making. The alternative would be "all sorts of quibbling." In other words, it will be necessary to appeal to rationalizations and justifications that, Tertullian thinks, would be an offense to God. Further, at the conclusion of the passage, he explicitly recognizes that a high cost might be involved for such obedience to Christian character—one might suffer martyrdom.

The suggestion that a person might suffer martyrdom for refusing to take up the sword was hardly an idle gesture or exaggeration on Tertullian's part. There are records of Christians who were killed for refusing the sword. Consider the case of Maximilian:

> In A.D. 295 Maximilian, a young Christian, was brought before the proconsul of Africa as fit for military service. He refused because he was a Christian: "I cannot serve as a soldier; I cannot do evil; I am a Christian." He was told there were other Christians in the legions and was asked what evil they did, but his decision was unchanged. When threatened with death he replied: "I cannot fight if I die." His death followed soon afterwards.[10]

Or, the case of Marinus:

> In Caesarea in A.D. 260 an officer named Marinus was about to be promoted to the rank of centurion, but was denounced as a Christian by another claimant. He was given three hours for reflection, and then returned from an interview with the bishop, who told him he must choose between his sword and the Gospels. He reaffirmed his faith and was beheaded.[11]

Tertullian's option—better martyrdom than to participate in warmaking—was no empty challenge, and as we see, some felt it better to be a martyr than to embrace the sword.

In addition to Tertullian, a number of the early fathers joined the assessment that following Jesus was inconsistent with participation in war. The reasons were usually the same—their understanding of the Lord's statements and the model that Jesus had set for them. Consider the early church theologian and martyr, rightly named Justin Martyr (A.D. 100–165):

> We, who had been filled with war and mutual slaughter and every wickedness, have each one—all the world over—changed the instruments of war, the swords into ploughs and the spears into farming implements, and we cultivate piety, righteousness, love for men, faith, and the hope which is from the Father Himself through the Crucified One.[12]

Irenaeus (130–c. 202) also claims that, in Christ, the prophecies of Micah and Isaiah are fulfilled and that instruments of war have been transformed into instruments for farming. Hippolytus (170–235) reminds us more of what we have seen from Tertullian. In *The Testament of our Lord* he writes:

> But if they [soldiers or those in authority] wish to be baptized in the Lord, let them cease from military service or from authority, and if not let them not be received. Let . . . a believer . . . if he desire to be a soldier, either cease from his intention, or if not let him be rejected. For he hath despised his God by his thought, and leaving the things of the Spirit, he hath perfected himself in the flesh, and hath treated the faith with contempt.[13]

In *The Apostolic Tradition,* Hippolytus writes:

> A military man in authority must not execute men. If he is ordered, he must not carry it out. Nor must he take military oath. If he refuses, he shall be rejected.[14]

Reminiscent of Tertullian, indeed, perhaps Hippolytus states the case even more strongly. There were yet others who argued that hands that took the Lord's Supper should not also be hands that shed blood. At any rate, most held that Christian faith was not consistent with participation in war.[15]

Origen's primary contributions to the issue of the Christian's participation in war appeared in *Contra Celsus.* Here is one example:

> To those who ask us whence we have come or whom we have for a leader, we say that we have come in accordance with the counsels of Jesus to cut down our warlike and arrogant swords of argument into ploughshares, and we convert into sickles the spears we formerly used in fighting. For we no longer take "sword against a nation," nor do we learn "any more to make war," having become sons of peace for the sake of Jesus, who is our leader, instead of following the ancestral customs in which we were strangers to the covenants.[16]

And, finally, Lactantius (260–340):

> When God prohibits killing, He not only forbids us to commit brigandage, which is not allowed even by the public laws; but He warns us that not even those things that are regarded as legal among men are to be done. And, so it will not be lawful for a just man to serve as a soldier—for justice itself is his military service—nor to accuse anyone of a capital offence, because it makes no difference whether thou kill with a sword or with a word, since killing itself is forbidden. And so, in this commandment of God, no exception at all ought to be made that it is always wrong to kill a man, whom God has wished to be a sacrosanct creature.[17]

Further readings from this period support the rejection of Christian participation in war, and the conclusion is clear: prior to Constantine, the church largely viewed participation in war as inconsistent with Christian faith. And, prior to 200, the rejection of Christian participation in war was overwhelming. The question, though, is what do we do with this information? How do we as

Christians in the twenty-first century, Christians who overwhelmingly support some version of just war theory, learn from the earliest thinkers in church history on these matters?

I do not know of any studies that attempt to compare the number of Christians who are pacifists with the number who are supporters of just war. I can only repeat what we have already noted: contemporary Christians are overwhelmingly supporters of just war, many rejecting Christian pacifism as both unwise and unsafe. In fact, it is likely that the vast majority of Christians since Augustine's time have been supporters of just war. This contrasts sharply with the early church period where the situation was quite the reverse, with the vast majority assuming that participation in war was inappropriate for Christians. While the precise reasons for the difference are uncertain, and probably such that we can never know for sure, different scholars have suggested reasons for it. I will not be exhaustive, but let's consider a few possibilities.

First, it has been suggested that the early church's objection to military service had more to do with the fact that some aspects of military service seemed to involve idolatry. The early Romans considered the emperor to be divine. Since Christians could only swear allegiance to the one God and Father of our Lord Jesus, the oath of office a soldier had to take could seem to affirm another god, involving the Christian soldier in idolatry. Coupled with the oath of allegiance, soldiers were often required to make sacrifice to the Roman gods in hopes of currying their favor for the battle. In addition, they were required to participate in rituals and to wear uniforms that Christians took to be either immoral or idolatrous or both. Of the reasons the early church spoke strongly against Christian participation in war, the idolatrous and pagan practices involved with military service were clearly a part. However, just as one cannot deny these concerns as part of the prohibition on serving in the Roman army, likewise, one cannot conclude that this is the only or primary concern. Too often terms like *blood shedding*, *killing*, and *torture* are used to describe the nature of the objection to participation in war. As Walter Wink notes, "If the church's sole objection to military service was idolatry, why do some of the fathers categorically forbid soldiers to kill?"[18] So, while we can affirm that idolatrous practices were a reason for the early Christians to resist becoming a part of the empire's military machine, it would be overly simplistic to assume that was the sole reason.

Defenders of just war theory occasionally look past writings from the early church that are similar to the ones cited above. Instead, they focus attention on the fact that, even before 200, there were Christians who did participate in military service. Of course, that this is so does not really prove very much. Does the fact that contemporary Christians participate in a variety of the common sins flesh is heir to lead us to conclude that church teaching approves those sins? Roland Bainton goes further, though, in his assessment of the reasons why some early Christians might have embraced being a part of the Roman army. During the early church period, there was no distinction between the police and the army. In times of peace, the Roman army also served as the local police. During times of war, their role switched and they became soldiers and warriors. As Bainton notes, the early church did not object to the existence of the state nor did it object to the ordering role that the police play during times of peace. Throughout the first few centuries, peace tended to prevail, except at the boundaries of the empire. It would have been quite possible for a person to serve their entire life in the Roman army, but never be called into battle and never be called upon to kill another. Under these terms, military-as-police service by Christians was acceptable. If, however, war should break out, the Christian was to refuse to participate. Martin of Tours was an example that Bainton notes, as he "remained in the army for two years, until an actual battle was imminent, and only then declined longer to serve."[19]

Again, this solution may not be adequate alone to explain the change in attitude toward war. It might, though, help one to see how participation in the Roman military, and ultimately in war, could have evolved over time. Christians believe in an orderly state of affairs, and they stood ready to participate in the police activities that made that possible. Since the police work did not involve war-making under most conditions, there was no conflict. Initially, when war broke out, as we saw above with Martin of Tours, Christians accepted martyrdom rather than service. One can imagine participation in the "military as police" slowly migrating to fuller participation, even after the outbreak of war. This seems particularly likely when seen in light of the increased involvement between church and state under Constantine.

Finally, turning our attention fully to the transformation under Constantine, it has been argued that the change of perspective regarding Christian participation in war was largely a result of the new role the church occupied after the Edict of Milan. Prior to that, Christians were largely a rag-tag group existing on the margins of society. They had little, if any, political power. So, there was no need for them to think through the complex issues relating to the Christian's participation in empire and its defense. However, after Constantine welcomed them into the halls of power, Christians found it necessary to think through what the new relationship meant, for the church as a whole and for individual Christians. They now exercised a moral influence on the state, and they scurried to develop the theological tools to take this responsibility seriously. To those who hold this position, Augustine's work on the just war theory was a great step forward in adding a moral dimension to a particularly nasty part of the life of the empire—war. What Augustine achieved (or at least launched) was an effort to think through what it meant for the church now to be "in power" rather than "out of power." JWTs, then, would not find the change from the pacifism of the early church so much a surprise as a necessary consequence of its new role.

Of course, Christian pacifists would agree with this analysis to a point. They would likely agree that this was precisely what Augustine was trying to do. They would object, however, that the move from "out of power" to "in power" was itself a betrayal of their Lord's commands and the church's status as "resident aliens"—a people occupying one space, but with their citizenship in another.

So, given that both sides provide what they believe to be plausible accounts of the changes, what are we to do with the strong words of the early church regarding Christian participation in war? I suggest two things. First, apart from whether we are persuaded to take up the position of the early church, it does us good to remind ourselves from time to time that we have Christian brothers and sisters who saw the world very differently than we do. We ought to ask ourselves why that is, and we ought to reflect on what we can learn from them. Perhaps, in this case, we can learn a bit more healthy skepticism about the justifications of a particular war and about claims that a given military action is warranted. Second, it is an interesting fact that of all the demographics in contemporary America, the people most likely to support a decision to go to war are white, evangelical Christians. Even if we do not come to agreement with the early church, perhaps we could come to agree that those who follow the one who was identified as the Prince of Peace should be the hardest to persuade to go to war, and not the easiest.

IX.

Early Christians in the Desert

One of my favorite Christian musicians was Rich Mullins, who was killed in an automobile accident in September of 1997 at the age of forty-one. Although I knew of his work prior to his death, I did not become a serious fan until after. Once I began to look into his music, I discovered that he had written many of the songs I had heard performed by other Christian artists between the late 1970s and his death. I bet you have also heard a song or two written by Rich Mullins, even if someone else performed it. In my case, as I got drawn more into Mullins's music, I found myself increasingly curious about how this Christian brother lived his life.

Mullins's father was a farmer in Indiana, and his mother was part of the Quaker tradition. He grew up attending a Friends' meetinghouse near his home. Not surprisingly, themes of social justice and peace often made their way into his music. The stories of his concerts are both unique and frequently heartwarming. For example, prior to a performance at one church, members planned a dinner for attendees to the concert. When folks arrived, they were greeted and served dinner by a barefooted Mullins. That he was the honored guest and performer for the evening did not change his desire to serve Christ through serving others.

In another case, a young woman tells the story of how she was dragged by her friend to a Mullins concert. Allegedly, she was a nonbeliever and was on the front porch of the church when Mullins came out for a breath of fresh air before his performance started. She did not recognize him. He started a conversation with her and asked her if she was looking forward to the concert. She said she did not figure she would enjoy it much and had been dragged there, rather unwillingly, by a friend. Mullins smiled and said that he hoped she would be surprised and enjoy it. Imagine her shock when she saw her chatting partner take the stage, introduced as the performer for the evening. As I understand it, the two stayed in touch after the concert, and the young woman later became a follower of Jesus. Stories of unconventional ways that he influenced others are legion. One other aspect of Mullins's life captured my attention, though, something that ran so counter to our normal way of thinking that it left me deeply moved.

After his death, friends put together a collection of some videos of Rich performing, interspersed with interviews of Mullins and his friends. One of them recounted a conversation in which the person interviewed indicated that he had asked Rich one question that is often considered rude, even between friends: how much money did he make on the royalties from his many popular songs? Mullins responded that he really did not know. When the friend looked at him strangely, he indicated that the royalty checks went to a group at his church who served as his advisors and accountability partners. Long ago, he had decided he would take from his earnings only the average salary for an American male for that year. The rest was given away to the poor and to various charities. Shortly before his death, this fan of St. Francis of Assisi described Christian faith this way:

> Jesus said whatever you do to the least of these, my brothers, you've done it to me. And this is what I've come to think. That if I want to identify fully with Jesus Christ, who I claim to be my Savior and Lord, the best way that I can do that is to identify with the poor. This I know will go against the teachings of all the popular evangelical preachers. But they're just wrong. They're not bad, they're just wrong. Christianity is not about building an absolutely secure little niche in the world where you can live with your perfect little wife and your perfect little children in a beautiful little house where you have no gays or minority groups anywhere near you. Christianity is about learning to love like Jesus loved and Jesus loved the poor and Jesus loved the broken . . . [concert recording cuts off at this moment, losing any further context for this particular quotation].[1]

Mullins describes two options for us: one, to enjoy the comforts that we normally take for granted as our right, or two, take up the same social location alongside the poor as Jesus did. He is crystal clear about the option he chose and why, and those who take the time to look into his life will discover the various ways he sought to live out those commitments.

Any study of the writings of the early fathers must explore the lifestyles and practices that some of them adopted in daily life. My goal is not to hold up the example of Rich Mullins as a standard to which all Christians should conform. Instead, I want us to examine the lengths to which some of our Christian brothers and sisters have gone in their attempt to be faithful witnesses of the impact following Jesus had on their lives. Sadly, as we noted in an earlier chapter, we live in an age when Christians exhibit very little by way of different behaviors from those of the non-Christians who live around us. In our study of the early church, we have certainly seen some differences that undoubtedly sound more than strange to us. In this chapter, I expect we will find the strangest so far. Yet, we can all be strengthened in our lives of discipleship if we ponder these behaviors and allow God to speak to us through them. I encourage your openness and invite you to reflect upon these "strange" early fellow Christians.

This chapter focuses on a particular set of Christians from the early church known as the desert fathers and mothers. These were persons who felt the need to live in a more monastic setting, often in solitude or semi-solitude. We still have such brothers and sisters in the world today. While those receiving such a call are a minority, we ought to allow their lives to speak to us. Perhaps we should be particularly attentive, just because the way they chose to live out their lives of faith stands in such strong distinction from our own. For the stories in this chapter, I am indebted primarily to three different sources: *The Wisdom of the Desert*, translated and introduced by Thomas Merton;[2] *The Wisdom of the Desert*, by James Hannay;[3] and *The Wisdom of the Desert Fathers and Mothers*, edited by Henry Carrigan.[4] Let us begin with a story from the life of Abbot Anastasius, from the collection by Merton:

> Abbot Anastasius had a book written on very fine parchment which was worth eighteen pence, and had in it both the Old and New Testaments in full. Once a certain

> brother came to visit him, and seeing the book made off with it. So that day when Abbot Anastasius went to read his book, and found that it was gone, he realized that the brother had taken it. *But he did not send after him to inquire about it for fear that the brother might add perjury to theft.* [emphasis mine] Well, the brother went down into the nearby city in order to sell the book. And the price he asked was sixteen pence. The buyer said: Give me that book that I may find out whether it is worth that much. With that, the buyer took the book to the holy Anastasius and said: Father, take a look at this book, please, and tell me whether you think I ought to buy it for sixteen pence. Is it worth that much? Abbot Anastasius said: Yes, it is a fine book, it is worth that much. So the buyer went back to the brother and said: Here is your money. I showed the book to Abbot Anastasius and he said it is a fine book and is worth at least sixteen pence. But the brother asked: Was that all he said? Did he make any other remarks? No, said the buyer, he did not say another word. Well, said the brother, I have changed my mind and I don't want to sell this book after all. Then he hastened to Abbot Anastasius and begged him with tears to take back his book, but the Abbot would not accept it, saying: Go in peace, brother, I make you a present of it. But the brother said: If you do not take it back I shall never have any peace. After that the brother dwelt with Abbot Anastasius for the rest of his life.[5]

I have italicized the words from the quotation that have haunted me for years—I know of no other way to say it. What would you or I do in a similar situation? I expect that once we realized the book was missing, we would take steps to get it back. After all, theft is wrong and there is nothing wrong with catching and punishing a thief. At least, that's how most of us think. Our brother, Abbot

Anastasius, though, was more concerned about the sins the thief was piling up with his behaviors. Why did the Abbot say nothing? Because he feared it would put the brother who stole the book in the position of needing to lie about his thievery, and thus, as the story says, "add perjury to theft." Anastasius thought it better to give up his book than to create a situation that would only make the brother sin more. Better to give up his prized copy of the Bible, according to Anastasius, than to have the brother lie about how the book came into his possession.

There is a similar story about robbers who broke into a monastery to take whatever things of value they could find. Here is that account:

> Once some robbers came into the monastery and said to one of the elders: We have come to take away everything that is in your cell. And he said: My sons, take all you want. So they took everything they could find in the cell and started off. But they left behind a little bag that was hidden in the cell. The elder picked it up and followed after them, crying out: My sons, take this, you forgot it in the cell! Amazed at the patience of the elder, they brought everything back into his cell and did penance, saying: This one really is a man of God.[6]

In this case, the robbers are more direct than in the story of Abbot Anastasius. They just come in and tell the elder they are taking everything. Not only does the elder welcome them to take all they want, but he chases them down when he discovers that they overlooked an item! A friend of mine once commented that the best security system to protect against robbers breaking into your home was simply not to have anything worth breaking in to steal.

Well, in this case, the elder had precious little, yet the robbers were so desperate, or so greedy, that they had not even the scruples to resist taking what little bit he did have. His detachment from his possessions was so great, however, that he simply did not resist the robbers. Was he pondering the passage "Resist not one who is evil" as he followed the course of action he did? Or, was his love for the robbers so great that he was glad for them to take whatever they needed? We will likely never know; all we have is this record of his action.

Both of these stories end well. In the first case, the brother who stole the book repented of his sin, ended up trying to make restitution, and then took up life alongside the good abbot. The brother gave up a life of crime for a life of discipleship at the feet of Abbot Anastasius. In the second story, we are told that the robbers brought back what they took and did penance. Of course, neither the abbot nor the elder had any way of knowing this would be the case when they did as they chose. In other words, both did what they did because they felt that love for their dishonest brothers dictated their course of action. You and I may disagree, but we would do well to consider the sort of detachment from possessions that Anastasius and the elder enjoyed and to ponder the implications for how we engage with those around us. As we think through these stories, it is hard not to recall the story of Jean Valjean and the bishop from Hugo's *Les Miserables.* When the authorities brought Valjean and the stolen silver back to the bishop, the bishop told them that he had given the objects to Valjean. Similar to the case of the second story above, he even brought forward some more items, saying that Valjean had forgotten to take them. Of course, some would say that if we all acted like Anastasius and the unnamed elder, the world would soon be overrun by thieves. Perhaps; perhaps not.

In the case of Serapion, the loss of his book was not from robbery, but rather because he felt he had learned how the value of the book could be better invested:

> One of the monks, a certain Serapion, possessed a copy of the gospels. This he sold and gave the price of it to the poor and hungry. Then he went home rejoicing, saying to himself, "Lo! now I have sold even that very book which was forever saying to me, Sell all that thou hast and give to the poor.[7]

Most of us read the command that Jesus gives to the rich young ruler, which appears in the first three Gospels, and simply observe that the command is given to the rich young ruler and not to us. However, Serapion would not let himself off the hook so easily. As a monk, he had already divested himself of the vast majority of the possessions he might have owned. Here, he makes what must seem to us a very serious sacrifice—he takes his copy of the Gospels and sells it. And why does he do that? So that he might care for the poor. I find his comment particularly poignant—he did with the book what the book told him to do.

Detachment from the wealth of the world is repeated often in these stories. Let's take a quick look at a couple more before we move on. First, consider the abbot who tells his monks that they should not own anything that they would have a hard time giving away:

> Abbot Agatho frequently admonished his disciple[s], saying: Never acquire for yourself anything that you might

> hesitate to give to your brother if he asked you for it, for thus you would be found a transgressor of God's command. If anyone asks, give to him, and if anyone wants to borrow from you, do not turn away from him.[8]

For these monks, there was no higher priority than their relationship with God. To allow any earthly possessions to get in the way of that relationship or to become an obstacle to complete obedience to God would be nothing short of idolatry. Now, consider the somewhat longer story of the wealthy man who decides to make a gift to the monks:

> A great noble whom nobody knew came to Scete bringing with him gold, and he asked the priest of that place to hand it out to the brethren. The priest said to him: The brethren don't need any of this. The nobleman insisted and would not take no for an answer; so he put the basket of gold down at the entrance to the church and said to the priest: Those who want some can help themselves. But no one touched any of the gold, and some did not even look at it. Then the elder said to the nobleman: The Lord has accepted your offering. Go, now, and give it to the poor.[9]

Sadly, later on, the monasteries would not as easily turn down the offer of gifts from wealthy benefactors. This is one of the reasons for the periodical reform movements that arose in the course of monastic history. It serves as a powerful reminder to us about what Jesus called "the deceitfulness of riches" that even those who had withdrawn into the monastic setting regularly fell prey to the temptation of material goods. In this particular case, though, the brothers justified their priest's confidence in them. They had no interest in the gold the wealthy man had offered them. But, note, rather than telling the rich man merely to keep his gold, he tells him that God has accepted it . . . for distribution to the poor!

If you take the time to read through all of the stories from the desert fathers, one thing you will find striking is the seriousness with which they took their own sins. Rather than looking to excuse their sins, they often seemed painfully aware of their own inability to escape the various sins that, as Paul wrote, so easily beset us. St. Moses the Black was a Coptic Christian who, prior to his conversion to Christian faith, was a slave of a government official. A large and imposing figure, he was once suspected of robbery and murder and was subsequently dismissed by his owner. Between his dismissal and his conversion, he headed a band of marauders who robbed and plundered as they chose. Once while trying to escape the authorities, he chose to hide among a group of monks. They so deeply influenced him that he ultimately gave up his life of crime and became a Christian. Since he was converted by the lives of the monks, he took up the monastic life himself. Others say that he strove for Christian perfection with the same zeal with which he had robbed and plundered. Here is a story from later in his life that shows how he responded to the call of his community to judge a brother who had been caught in sin (to make the point about his zeal for conversion of life and his reluctance to judge another, I juxtapose two different short stories of St. Moses):

> Moses was torn up by lustful, angry, and violent thoughts in his early career. He could not shake his past spiritually. After years of struggle he was released from his past when, attending to confession with St. Macarius, he saw an angel wiping the slate clean of his past transgressions. After this vision, he was free at last, and thus his life in Christ

> deepened. His brother monks respected him because of his wisdom, his humility, and his asceticism.[10]

Then, the story of being called to judge another:

> A brother in Scete happened to commit a fault, and the elders assembled and sent for Abbot Moses to join them. He, however, did not want to come. The priest sent him a message, saying, "Come, the community of the brethren is waiting for you." So he arose and started off. And taking with him a very old basket full of holes, he filled it with sand, and carried it behind him. The elders came out to meet him, and said, "What is this, father?" The [abbot] replied, "My sins are running out behind me, and I do not see them, and today I come to judge the sins of another!" They, hearing this, said nothing to the brother but pardoned him.[11]

In Luke 7 the Lord reminds us that those who are forgiven often respond with deeper love. He said this in response to the woman who knelt at his feet, anointed them with oil, and wiped them dry with her hair. St. Moses was obviously a man of great passion and one who brought with him to the monastery a wretched past. As he sought more and more to draw close to God, past sins increasingly weighed him down. But after the vision of his sins being forgiven, he felt empowered to live the life he desired. Perhaps, then, his unwillingness to judge another arose from his own experiences of how God, rather than punishing him, had brought him to the brothers so that he might learn from them. Even though the second story comes later than the first, notice that Moses is still painfully aware of his many sins—so many and so hard to track that he chose the basket, constantly leaking sand, as an object lesson for his brothers. While, of course, Jesus did not have sins to worry about as did Moses, one cannot help thinking of the woman caught in adultery. It was after reminding the others present of their own sins that Jesus pronounced her sins forgiven.

Perhaps one of the stranger things we find among the early desert fathers was a frequent unwillingness to respond to accusations. This story of Macarius is hard for us to fathom—why would a Christian react to these charges as he did?

> At some point, Macarius abandoned camel-driving and became an ascetic living on the fringe of his village, much as the young Antony once had. When villagers went to force him to become a cleric, he fled to another village. Sometime after he had settled there, a young girl accused him of getting her pregnant. The villagers were incensed. They barged into his hermitage, beat him, dragged him around the village, and, in a gesture meant to signal his disgrace, hung soot blackened pots around his neck. The girl's parents demanded Macarius pay support for their daughter and for the future baby. Strangely, he did not deny the charge, even though it was false. Instead he said to himself, "Macarius, you have found yourself a wife; you must work a little more in order to keep her." So he wove baskets and sent the earnings to his "wife." When it came time for the girl to have the baby, she went into labor, but it went on and on for days. She was unable to give birth. Finally, in desperation, she admitted that it was not Macarius who had gotten her pregnant, but a young man from the area. So the villagers who had slandered and beaten Macarius decided to come and do penance before him. On learning of this he fled.[12]

As is often the case in these stories from the desert fathers, the offended party is vindicated in the end. Here, the woman who falsely accused Macarius confessed in the late stages of a long and painful delivery. Yet, Macarius could easily have denied the charges. The fact that a local village had tried to make him a priest would at least suggest he would have been successful in repudiating the claim that he fathered this woman's child. Did he do what he did out of pity for the pregnant woman? Out of concern for the unborn child? Or, perhaps there was no other genuine path of vindication than the one Macarius chose?

In addition to remaining quiet in the face of false charges, there are several stories of how the desert fathers and mothers disciplined themselves not to respond to insults. Consider:

> There was a certain elder who, if anyone maligned him, would go in person to offer him presents, if he lived nearby. And if he lived at a distance he would send presents by the hand of another.[13]

"Count it as joy to be maligned for the gospel." Do you suppose this is the passage this brother had in mind as he undertook the strange habit of rewarding those who spoke evil of him? Jesus did say that we should rejoice and be happy when we were insulted for his sake. Here is another example that goes into more detail:

> Once there was a disciple of a Greek philosopher who was commanded by his Master for three years to give money to everyone who insulted him. When this period of trial was over, the Master said to him: Now you can go to Athens and learn wisdom. When the disciple was entering Athens he met a certain wise man who sat at the gate insulting everybody who came and went. He also

> insulted the disciple who immediately burst out laughing. "Why do you laugh when I insult you?" said the wise man. "Because," said the disciple, "for three years I have been paying for this kind of thing and now you give it to me for nothing." "Enter the city," said the wise man, "it is all yours." Abbot John used to tell the above story, saying, "This is the door of God by which our fathers rejoicing in many tribulations enter into the City of Heaven."[14]

How easily we are distracted when someone insults us. We become angry with the one insulting us. Too easily, getting even with the person for the insult becomes an obsession for us, occupying our minds and distracting us from what would be more proper objects of our contemplation. I recall a conversation with a colleague who told me of some particular innuendos that he had received at the hands of another. I was aghast and asked how he had responded. His answer bore an interesting resemblance to what we see here. He said, "I gave thanks to God for him. I am not a patient man, and I assumed God sent him to me to teach me patience." It is worth considering the benefits of being more immune to the insults we often have to bear.

How do you respond to insults, particularly unwarranted ones? Too often, my response bears more resemblance to this brother than to the last one:

> One of the brethren had been insulted by another and he wanted to take revenge. He came to Abbot Sisois and told him what had taken place, saying: I am going to get even, Father. But the [abbot] besought him to leave the affair in the hands of God. No, said the brother, I will not give up until I have made that fellow pay for what he said. Then the [abbot] stood up and began to pray in these terms:

> O God, Thou art no longer necessary to us, and we no longer need Thee to take care of us since, as this brother says, we both can and will avenge ourselves. At this the brother promised to give up his idea of revenge.[15]

By now, I suspect you can see how often the desert fathers' behaviors are implicitly connected to what the Scriptures model for followers of Jesus. Here, we are put in mind of Romans 12 where Paul quotes the Lord as saying, "Revenge belongs to me; I will pay it back" (verse 19). Notice how wisely the abbot responds to the brother. First, he tries to talk him out of his determination to get even. When that fails, he prays, telling God that, since we can now handle our own affairs, we no longer need him! Happily, the brother is shamed into repentance.

So, what do we make of all this—detachment from riches, withdrawal from the world, rejoicing at being insulted, not responding to false charges? I wish I could conclude this chapter with three easy points for us to take away, but there is no such conclusion. I read through Merton's *Wisdom of the Desert* from time to time, just to remind myself that there are other Christians, from other times, who understood being faithful to God's call on our lives very differently than I do. I always walk away from these readings challenged, though not always challenged to imitate their specific acts. Instead, I am challenged to allow the gospel to more radically influence me, to let it reshape my values, to let it tear down the monument to myself that my life can so easily become. I often find myself walking away from the readings shaking my head, clearly moved, clearly challenged, but not so clear on what it all means. Maybe, just maybe, not knowing exactly is sometimes a good thing. . . . St. Anthony seemed to think so:

> Some elders once came to Abbot Anthony, and there was with them also Abbot Joseph. Wishing to test them, Abbot Anthony brought the conversation around to the Holy Scriptures. And he began from the youngest to ask them the meaning of this or that text. Each one replied as best he could, but Abbot Anthony said to them: You have not got it yet. After them all he asked Abbot Joseph: What about you? What do you say this text means? Abbot Joseph replied: I know not! Then Abbot Anthony said: Truly Abbot Joseph alone has found the way, for he replies that he knows not.[16]

When we think we know the meaning, the passage in question is often put out of our minds, added to the list of passages we have "mastered." Yet, when we admit that we have not yet gotten it, our minds remain attentive, inquisitive, and the passage cannot so easily be dismissed. Perhaps recognizing that we "do not know" actually creates a space within which the Holy Spirit can work. I am not arguing that the goal of the Christian is to "not know" how to live. However, our willingness to read and ponder things we do not yet grasp might well be a powerful point of access for God in his ongoing effort to transform our lives. Read, ponder, reflect, and be open. These are the words of encouragement I leave you as we finish our study. May God speak to us the words we each need to hear, and may his Spirit empower us to allow the radical call of the Galilean to have full sway in our lives!

NOTES

Introduction

1. George Barna, *The Second Coming of the Church* (Nashville: Thomas Nelson, 2001). See, for example, the later work by the current head of the Barna Group, David Kinnaman, *unChristian: What a New Generation Really Thinks about Christianity . . . and Why It Matters* (Grand Rapids: Baker Books, 2007).

1. Reading Scripture with the Early Church

1. Hans von Campenhausen, *The Formation of the Christian Bible* (Minneapolis: Fortress Press, 1972).

2. See http://www.ntcanon.org/Athanasius.shtml.

3. Ibid.

4. Ibid. I omit Athanasius's reference to apocryphal writings that he characterizes as "a fabrication of the heretics" for a couple of reasons. First and most important, what Athanasius has in mind with the term *apocryphal* is very different from the sense in which it is used later to reference the Apocrypha. This is obvious because he names books in the present-day Apocrypha as part of the "reading-matter" he references and because he quotes from them with approval. Second, we do not have space to engage all the writings that different persons in the early church considered authoritative. Instead, we note that the common sentiment that books worthy of our attention extend beyond the sixty-six canonical books.

5. John A. McGuckin, "Origen as Literary Critic in the Alexandrian Tradition," pp. 121-37 in vol. 1 of "Origeniana octava: Origen and the Alexandrian Tradition." Papers of the 8th International Origen Congress, edited by L. Perrone, 2 vols. (Leuven: Leuven University Press, 2003).

6. Origen, *On First Principles*, trans. G. W. Butterworth (Gloucester, Mass.: Peter Smith Publisher, 1973), pp. 275-76.

7. Ibid., pp. 277-78.

8. Ibid. See, for example, pp. 288-94.

9. Ibid., p. 294.

10. Ibid.

11. Ibid., p. 296.

12. Ibid., p. 297.

13. Yes, I am sure Origen would have recognized that all bring presuppositions to the text, but his goal was to minimize those to the extent possible, letting the Scriptures speak for themselves with the Spirit as guide.

14. Origen, *On First Principles*, pp. 285-87.

2. Unity and Schism in the Early Church

1. The issue was the so-called *filioque* clause in the creed. The question was the equal deity of the Father and the Son. The Eastern church held that the clause implied a subordinationist view of the Spirit in relation to the Father and the Son and divided from the Western church over the disagreement.

2. Indeed, how could I, given that I am a Protestant myself?

3. *The World Christian Encyclopedia*, published by Oxford Press in 2001 and compiled by David Barrett, for example, estimates the number of denominations at over thirty thousand.

4. Irenaeus, *Against Heresies*, Book I, Chapter 10. Available online at http://www.newadvent.org/fathers/0103110.htm.

5. Irenaeus, *Against Heresies*, Book IV, Chapter 33. Available online at http://www.newadvent.org/fathers/0103433.htm.

6. It is worth remembering that all of the writings of the early church were, of course, written prior to even the first great schism, the East/West split in 1054. So, it is not surprising that they all, in their strong defense of Christian unity, argue that the Roman Catholic Church is the one true church. We need not enter that debate, one in which I obviously stand on the other side. I will simply note that one need not agree that all Christians ought to be united under the Roman banner in order to conclude that the

current level of denominationalism and congregationalism, with some thirty thousand different denominations, has damaged the church more than it has helped.

7. St. Clement of Rome, "First Epistle to the Corinthians," ca. A.D. 96.

8. Hilary of Poitiers, *On the Trinity*, book 7, chapter 4. Available online at http://www.newadvent.org/fathers/330207.htm.

9. Cyprian of Carthage, Epistle 54. Available online at http://www.newadvent.org/fathers/050654.htm.

10. Cyprian of Carthage, Epistle 43. Available online at http://www.newadvent.org/fathers/050643.htm.

11. Dionysius, Letter 2 to Novatus. Available online at http://www.ccel.org/ccel/schaff/anf06.iv.iii.ii.ii.html.

12. St. John Chrysostom, *Second Homily on Eutropius*. Available online at http://www.newadvent.org/fathers/1915.htm.

13. Feel free to substitute another denomination, as the point is not a critique of this particular one.

3. Discipleship in the Early Church

1. Clinton Arnold, "Early Church Catechesis," *JETS*, 47:1 (Mar 2004).

2. *The Catechetical Oration of Gregory of Nyssa*, edited by James Herbert Strawley (Cambridge: The University Press, 1903).

3. Available online at http://www.ccel.org/ccel/schaff/npnf205.xi.ii.ii.html.

4. Cyril, Introduction to the *Catechetical Lectures*, section 11. Available online at http://www.newadvent.org/fathers/310100.htm.

5. Augustine, *On Catechising the Uninstructed*, section 1. Available online at http://www.newadvent.org/fathers/1303.htm.

6. Ibid., section 2.

7. Ibid., section 5.

8. Ibid., section 26.

9. *Apostolic Teaching*, Section 8, XXXII. Compare also *The Apostolic Tradition of Hippolytus of Rome*, which has very similar words in section 17.

4. The Early Fathers on Human Freedom

1. For detail, see my dissertation, *Reconsidering the Doctrine of God* (London: T & T Clark, 2005).

2. Paraphrased from remembered conversation.

3. For locating these quotations, I am indebted to the following website: http://www.angelfire.com/ab8/hobbes/antenicene.html.

4. Ibid.

5. Ibid.

6. Ibid.

7. Augustine, *The Confessions*, Book VIII, chapter 7. Available online at http://www.newadvent.org/fathers/110108.htm.

8. Ibid., chapter 12. A slightly different translation is available at the same address.

9. Available online at http://www.newadvent.org/fathers/1701041.htm.

10. Available online at http://www.newadvent.org/fathers/1302.htm.

11. Ibid.

12. Charles Gutenson, *Christians and the Common Good* (Grand Rapids: Brazos Press, 2011).

13. Bob Dylan, "You Gotta Serve Somebody," 1979.

5. *The Early Fathers on Wealth and Poverty*

1. http://en.wikipedia.org/wiki/Basil_of_Caesarea.

2. Basil the Great, *On Avarices.*

3. Ibid.

4. Ibid.

5. St. John Chrysostom, "Homily 7," *Homily on Romans.* Available online at http://www.newadvent.org/fathers/210207.htm.

6. Consider http://www.theburninghand.com/1/post/2011/3/turning-towards-justice.html.

7. Gregory of Nyssa, from "Homily 40."

8. John Chrysostom, a homily on the poor. Available online at http://www.christianitytoday.com/ch/1987/issue14/1410.html?start=4.

9. See http://www.njcathconf.com/content/social_justice_poverty.php.

10. Irenaeus, *Against Heresies*, IV, xiii, 3. A slightly different version is available online at http://www.newadvent.org/fathers/0103413.htm.

11. Leo the Great, "Homily on Matthew 25."

6. *Stewardship of Creation*

1. Already in the book of Genesis, we find such problems. Consider for example the great famine that relocated the Israelites to Egypt.

2. See http://en.wikipedia.org/wiki/600 for example.

3. The entire document can be found at http://www.scribd.com/doc/45307006/Krueger-creation-care-quotes-Ecological-Legacy-of-Christianity.

4. So called to distinguish him from Clement of Alexandria, to whom we will soon turn attention.

5. Clement's letter to the Corinthians; see Krueger, *A Cloud of Witnesses*, p. 25.

6. Irenaeus, *Against Heresies.* Available online at http://www.gnosis.org/library/advh2.htm.

7. Krueger, *A Cloud of Witnesses*, p. 37.

8. Clement of Alexandria, *Christ the Educator*, book 2, chapter 1, p. 93.

9. Ibid., and passim pp. 94-110.

10. Ibid., book 2. See Krueger, *A Cloud of Witnesses*, p. 39.

11. Krueger, *A Cloud of Witnesses*, p. 49.

12. Marcus Minucius Felix, *The Octavius*, XVIII. A slightly different version is available online at http://www.newadvent.org/fathers/0410.htm.

13. St. John Chrysostom, Homily XXXIX, 35, Commentary on the Epistle to the Romans.

14. Chrysostom, *On the Creation of the World*, v. 7. See Krueger, *A Cloud of Witnesses*, p. 147.

7. Society and Government

1. That is, to our personal, nonpublic lives.

2. See Stanley Hauerwas, *A Community of Character: Toward a Constructive Christian Social Ethic* (Notre Dame, Ind.: University of Notre Dame Press, 1991), chapter 4, pp. 72-86.

3. I am not arguing that people cannot be moral apart from religion, but rather that religious discipline has consistently, from a historical perspective, served an important role in moral training and apprenticing.

4. It should give us some pause that the Scriptures reference this as "each person [doing] what they thought to be right," and it is uniformly considered to be a bad thing. Consider, for example, Judges 21:25.

5. Hauerwas, *A Community of Character*, p. 79.

6. Ibid.

7. I cannot help noting here the contemporary popularity of the works of Ayn Rand, sadly, even amongst those who self-identify as followers of Jesus. According to Rand, an avowed atheist, the maximization of

personal liberty to do as one pleases, with minimal restraint, is the greatest good for humans. In such a world, according to Rand, charity becomes a bad thing and leaving the poor and marginalized to fend for themselves as best they can is precisely the sort of "tough love" we should all embody. For those wanting to delve into more detail, consider her work *Atlas Shrugged.*

8. Hauerwas, *A Community of Character*, p. 74.

9. Tertullian, "Apoligeticum," chapter 50.

10. St. Ignatius, "Letter to the Romans," available online at http://www.suscopts.org/stgeorgetampa/Letter_to_Romans.html.

11. Reported in a letter from the Church of Smyrna, available online at http://www.newadvent.org/cathen/12219b.htm.

12. To do so was considered idolatry and a turning away from Christian faith.

13. Reported in a letter from the Church of Smyrna, available online at http://www.newadvent.org/cathen/12219b.htm.

14. Quoted in Robert L. Wilkin, "The Piety of the Persecutors," *Christian History*, Issue 27 (Vol. IX, No. 3), p. 19.

15. Ibid.

16. Ibid.

17. Ibid.

18. Tertullian, *Apology*, chapter 33; available online at http://www.newadvent.org/fathers/0301.htm.

19. Justin Martyr, *Apology* 1, chapter 17; available online at http://www.newadvent.org/fathers/0126.htm.

20. Tertullian, *Apology*, Chapter 35; available online at http://www.newadvent.org/fathers/0301.htm.

21. Theo-politics—the mixing together of theology (the study of God) with politics (the study of the welfare of the nation/state).

22. The quotation can be found online at http://en.wikipedia.org/wiki/Edict_of_Milan.

23. Robert W. Brimlow and Michael L. Budde, *Christianity Incorporated: How Big Business Is Buying the Church* (Eugene, Ore.: Wipf and Stock, 2007). Note that Budde and Brimlow characterize the church as chaplain to capitalism. I merely borrow their way of defining the role of chaplain.

24. See chapter 4 for a more detailed examination of the different kinds of freedom Christians have been and should be concerned about.

8. The Early Church on War

1. Consider, for example, that one would not quote Old Testament rules about sacrifice to justify a need for offering sacrifices today. The life of Jesus changed much, and Augustine should have given us an explanation of why the Christian participation in war was not one of those changed realities. This is particularly pressing in light of Jesus' own pronouncements.

2. St. Thomas Aquinas, *Summa Theologica,* Second Part of the Second Part, Question 40; available online at http://www.newadvent.org/summa/3040.htm.

3. Ibid.

4. Though Jerome claims Tertullian lived to a great age, there is no evidence of his work beyond 220.

5. Tertullian, *On Idolatry,* 19. A slightly different version is available online at http://www.newadvent.org/fathers/0302.htm.

6. Tertullian, *De Corona,* chapter 11. Available online at http://www.newadvent.org/fathers/0304.htm.

7. Ibid.

8. Ibid.

9. Ibid.

10. Edgar W. Orr, *Christian Pacifism* (Essex, England: The C. W. Daniel Company, 1957), p. 69.

11. Ibid.

12. Justin Martyr, *Dialogue with Trypho,* 110. A slightly different version is available online at http://www.newadvent.org/fathers/01288.htm.

13. Hippolytus, *The Testament of Our Lord.* For a full version, see http://www.archive.org/details/cu31924029296170.

14. Hippolytus, *The Apostolic Tradition,* 16, 9.

15. It should be noted that there was no distinction between the military and the police in the early period. Christians seemed clearly to have a much stronger objection to any kind of killing (in war or in the course of policing) than to the orderly management of society in general. This might explain how, along with the changes under Constantine, Christians became more and more involved over time.

16. Origen, *Contra Celsus,* v. 33.

17. Lactantius, *Divine Institutes,* VI, 20, 15.

18. Walter Wink, *Engaging the Powers* (Minneapolis: Fortress Press, 1992), p. 211.

19. Roland H. Bainton, *Christian Attitudes toward War and Peace* (Nashville: Abingdon, 1960), p. 81.

9. Early Christians in the Desert

1. http://www.youtube.com/watch?v=vQnFU5JvuWY&mode=related&search= (the quoted speech begins at 7:40 of this video reference).

2. Thomas Merton, *The Wisdom of the Desert* (New York: New Directions, 1970).

3. James O. Hannay, *The Wisdom of the Desert* (Charlotte, N.C.: IAP, 2009).

4. Henry L. Carrigan, Jr., ed., *The Wisdom of the Desert Fathers and Mothers* (Brewster, Mass.: Paraclete Press, 2010).

5. Merton, *Wisdom of the Desert,* pp. 30-31.

6. Ibid., p. 59.

7. Hannay, *Wisdom of the Desert,* p. 100.

8. Merton, *Wisdom of the Desert,* p. 47.

9. Ibid., p. 57.

10. Find online at http://stanthonylc.org/article.php?id=2046.

11. Merton, *Wisdom of the Desert,* 29.

12. William Harmless, *Desert Christians: An Introduction to the Literature of Early Monasticism* (New York: Oxford University Press, 2004), p. 194.

13. Merton, *Wisdom of the Desert,* p. 48.

14. Ibid., p. 27.

15. Ibid., p. 26.

16. Ibid., p. 40.

CPSIA information can be obtained at www.ICGtesting.com
Printed in the USA
LVOW131311040812

292874LV00004B/1/P